Basemen+

Business has never been

so easy

Technical preface

These elements marked by nine symbols, their arrangement and relationship to each other, are called "the entrepreneur matrix" by the author. The Entrepreneur Matrix explains in detail throughout this book. The name Entrepreneur Matrix is composed of the words Entrepreneurship and Matrix. Entrepreneurship is an entrepreneurial mindset that is always looking for new opportunities. A matrix is a certain arrangement of elements. The Entrepreneur Matrix presents in this book and developed by the author makes it possible for the user to work in a defined manner to develop and manage his business successfully.

Table of contents

List of figures

1 <u>Introduction</u>

This book or the concept of the Entrepreneur Matrix explained here conveys a new, holistic understanding of entrepreneurship.

Based on a nine-field matrix, the interrelationships of the individual areas in business management quickly become transparent.

The context or the basic principle of entrepreneurship can also be quickly learned from later working life, for example as a manager, and quickly implemented.

In addition, one can perceive each company from a different perspective and approach projects successfully and self-confidently with this new knowledge.

Irrespective of how one's Personal life develops, whether in the company or in self-employment, the matrix structure helps to maintain an entrepreneurial overview.

Now to the Matrix. The Entrepreneur Matrix is one of the most effective and efficient (low-cost) tools for setting up and running a business. The Entrepreneur Matrix summarizes entrepreneurship in only 9 symbols!

It helps to successfully start a business and to keep the overview in existing businesses or to gain the overview.

The order created by the matrix minimizes the risk of failure of any company.

The Entrepreneur Matrix is equally suitable for service companies as well as for producing, non-profit or trading companies. It is also intended for academics and non-academics.

The basic concept is simple and explained in the shortest possible time. Individual implementation requires concentration and active thinking. It also concerns for taking responsibility. The more one gets an insight into management, the more one can take over responsibility. Responsibility means determining the process, looking for solutions perpetually and assuming what happens in case of failures. Everyone personally bears the responsibility for their actions. The ability to assume responsibility distinguishes a manager from "normal" employees.

Before we move on to the Matrix, there are a few important hints:

- The Entrepreneur Matrix does not replace legal advice (if it is used afterwards to find a company or is also used as a business tool in the company). Laws are constantly changing and are already a jungle without change. With patents, searches, trademarks and all other legal ambiguities, it always makes sense to rely on experts. The legal framework can otherwise quickly become a pitfall in the event of disregard or non-observance. The matrix is a country unspecific. Rights and laws must be adapted/applied individually according to the country. A few legal examples are described according to German law.

- If the Entrepreneur Matrix serves as a basic building block for a business plan that is intended for submission to banks or investors, it makes sense to have someone in the business (e.g. A management consultant) look at the finished work. A management consultant, etc., who already knows the bank/investor, can usually give very helpful tips. In this way, the business plan can be upgraded, and the chances of financing improved.

- The aim of the Entrepreneur Matrix is to develop a basic thinking module. It should also serve as a guideline. The sub-items of the guideline can be individually adapted and extended. The matrix can be applied to any business. It makes no claim to completeness of all theoretical models, concepts or strategies.

2 The Structure of the "Matrix"

This section explains the basic structure of the matrix. This section explains the basic logical structure of the fields. In the following chapters, all fields are analyzed and displayed individually.

The Entrepreneur Matrix consists of 9 fields. The fields are identified by symbols. The symbols can be used as a visual reminder.

A Matrix Field is explained by the remaining fields. This structure explains each field in the best possible way. The main field is therefore only the heading, since this is the reference point to the remaining sub-fields.

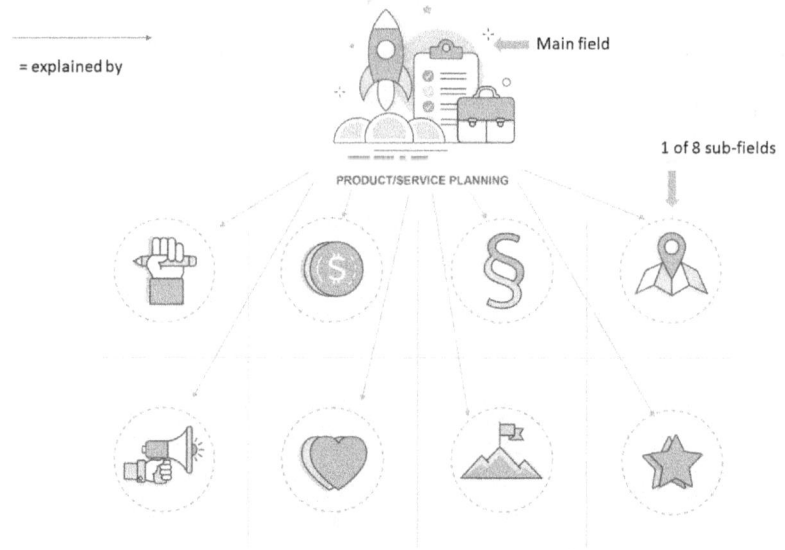

Figure 3 – The Matrix Field explained at Matrix Field 1

One of the remaining eight fields below is called a subfield by the matrix structure.

This also results in a naming by numbers. In this course the matrix fields are numbered with 2 numbers: e.g. 1.3 - the first number names the main field, the second number names the subfield.

A subfield always refers to the respective main field.

Three examples for the matrix designation by numbers:

• 1.6 - Advertising (6) in relation to the product/ service

Service planning (1)

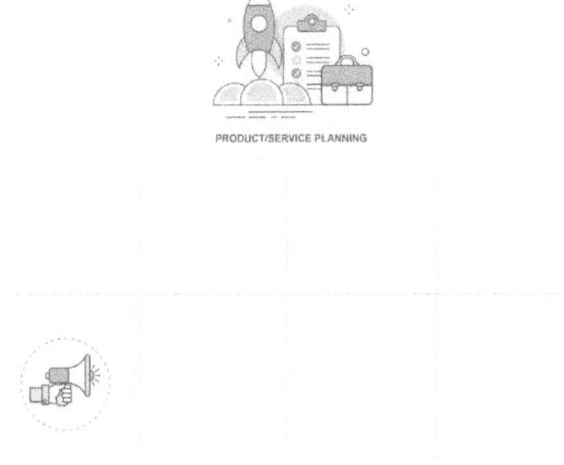

PRODUCT/SERVICE PLANNING

• 4.8 - Objective (8) in relation to the legal basis for the Framework of the enterprise (4)

LAW

- 9.5 - Platforms (5) for Improvements (9)

IMPROVEMENT

Field 1 - Product/service planning

PRODUCT/SERVICE PLANNING

The first symbol stands for product / service planning. This is the foundation stone for the company. Because the business idea is the result of an idea for a product or a service.

The position as the first field was chosen because without the product or service there would be no need to start a company or a project. A product or service is therefore the most important prerequisite for founding a company or starting a project. The development of this field results in a detailed product/service planning or description. A commercial enterprise must also pass through this field. Who does not know his product, no matter whether he produces it himself or not, cannot know the target group. Without customers who emerge from the target group, there is no turnover, no profit and thus a pre-programmed failure.

It is theoretically possible to press the "start button" after working through this field (and implementing the information obtained) so that the product is produced or the service is ready for implementation. In other words: Field 1 deals with everything that is important around the product/service.

By relating the sub-fields to the main field (here Field 1), possibilities are found as to how production could proceed or where the procurement of required goods could take place. The aim of the sub-fields of this field is to check whether the product/service has a fundamental chance on the market (suppliers and consumers meet on the market).

Field 2 – Strategic planning

STRATEGIC PLANNING

The pen stands for strategic planning.

The strategy is the plan that describes the future actions of the company - thus it is about strategies for all areas relevant to the company.

The position Field 2 was chosen because it takes up data from product and service planning and collects information for the financial plan. After a thorough review, it will become clear whether the company is promising. The strategy as well as the business idea is among the most important prerequisites for the foundation of a company or the start of a project.

All contents, which are in the field of strategic planning, together with the essential description factors from the Field 1 (product and service planning) and Field 3 (financial planning) result in the basic elements of a "normal" business plan.

Field 3 – Financial planning

FINANCIAL PLANNING

The dollar sign stands for the financial plan.

The position was chosen because the finance plan determines all costs relating to the product/service and the strategy. After working through this field, you will see whether there is sufficient capital (whether through equity, loans, or investors).

At this point an important hint:

Numbers are used for control purposes. The financial plan is an indispensable document for control. It shows costs, turnover and consequently profit. These factors and the resulting KPIs (Key Performance Indicators) show whether the company is still on course or not. The aim of the financial plan is to check whether the company or the project is possible and whether the financial resources are sufficient.

The planning phase ends with the financial planning. The matrix now passes into the implementation phase.

1: Planning phase

2: Implementation phase

Field 4 – Law

LAW

The symbol of the paragraph stands here for laws, rights, patents, contracts, the form of enterprise, etc., in summary the entire legal framework around a business.

The position of Field 4 was chosen because a business has to be registered before it can start selling.

Field 5 – Location

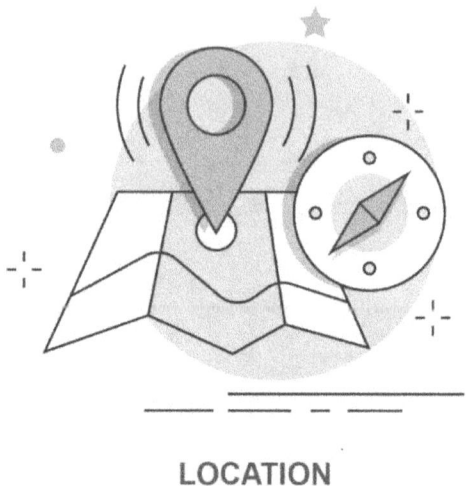

LOCATION

The most important places for a company are its Personal location/administration as well as the places of purchase and sale. In the manufacturing industry and also in some service industries, production halls and warehouses for complete distribution are added to the company's Personal location (depending on the literature, the word logistics are often used for distribution). Logistics includes the storage and delivery of products to a recipient (usually a customer).

This results in four possible important locations:

1. The branch office (includes at least its Personal administrative)

2. The production

3. The warehouse for logistics

4. The points of sale

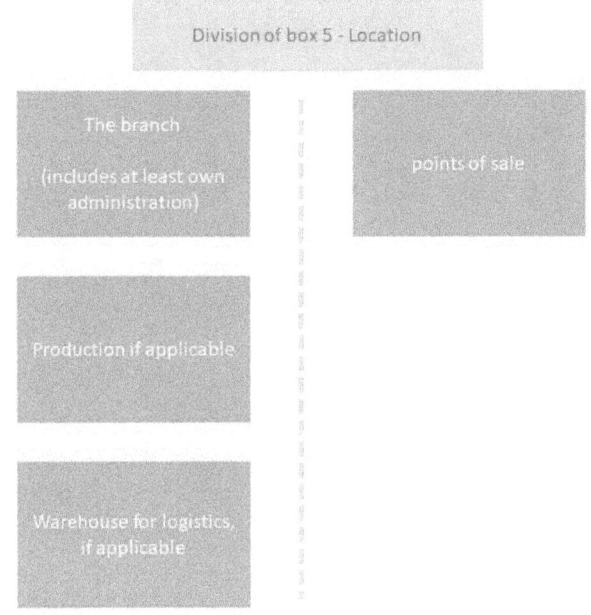

Websites and online platforms are also locations. A website is a virtual location where actions such as buying, selling, advertising, communicating, etc. are just as possible as at a physical (tangible) location.

The position of Field 5 was chosen because the place of distribution of a product or service usually influences how advertising is designed. Thus, this point directly follows the legal framework that symbolizes the permission to start the business.

Field 6 – Publicity

PUBLICITY

The megaphone stands for advertising.

Advertising is the announcement of a product/service on a market[1]. The advertiser communicates with the intention of conveying a positive and interesting image of the object (product or service) to be advertised. The aim is to bring about purchase decisions or the decision to use the service.

---

[1] Cf. Wolff 2008: 42.

Advertising thus creates an image of the advertised product/service among people and tries to turn those who hear and/or see the message into customers.

The position as Field 6 was chosen because the product/service is now accessible by selecting the points of sale. In order for the product/service to become visible, advertising is needed, since on almost every sales platform in the world a product/service is (almost) not seen without advertising.

This point contains points of the (partly) higher-level, but by definition different term, marketing. Marketing is an entrepreneurial mindset that specifically deals with the points of contact between the company, the target group or the interested parties and ultimately the customer in order to position the company as successful as possible on the market. [2] Marketing therefore exceeds pure advertising and is integrated into the matrix at various points. The field of advertising is a part of marketing.

---

[2] Cf. Meffert, Burmann, Kirchgeorg 2014: 10.

Field 7 – Human

HUMAN

The symbol stands for the human heart. Therefore, it symbolizes the human aspect of the enterprise. The people here are the personnel and the target group.

The position as Field 7 was chosen for the following reasons:

- With regard to the staff:

Growth, where personnel are needed, usually comes from turnover or increase in turnover, and therefore takes place only after the product/service has been made accessible and visible. The word personnel stand for the employees in the company who are needed to manufacture or provide a product or to be able to offer a service.

- With regard to the target group:

In order to refine the target group, experience is important. Without experience, there is no control over the objectives set for the target group. The experience can only be gathered when the product or service is available and advertising has been placed. Of course, the target group cannot be defined only at the end. This point is already found in the matrix in the first main field. Without a target group that is defined as precisely as possible, it is difficult to make decisions that appeal to the target group.

Field 8 - Goal

GOAL

The symbol represents a destination flag. Goals must be measurable and realistic. Measurable means that a company can define a target regionally, temporally and in another quantitative dimension such as turnover.

Controlling is closely linked to the objective. Controlling means taxes. In concrete terms, controlling is about success-oriented corporate management on the basis of objectives.

The area of controlling also includes accounting. In accounting, all quantifiable data (quantifiable data are measurable values) are recorded and evaluated as far as possible.

If a check shows that there are unwanted deviations, action must be taken. If necessary, the company's course must be adjusted in order to achieve the goal in the best possible way. The typical tasks of controlling also include drawing up budget plans and sales forecasts. Strategic measures are planned and implemented by Controlling. Controlling not only deals with new, specially created tasks, but also keeps an eye on established company processes. Processes are analyzed to optimize weak points. The Controlling department works closely with the management and delivers prepared results (figures) to the management. The reason for a close cooperation is the fact that the key figures show the course and its possible deviation of the company and that decisions have to be made accordingly.

The position of Field 8 was chosen because the achievement of objectives can only be verified if the steps planned to achieve the objectives (marketing plans, advertising plans, target group plans, etc.) have already been implemented.

Like all other points in the matrix, controlling and objectives are not only found in this field, but in this case are represented in each field by subfield 8.

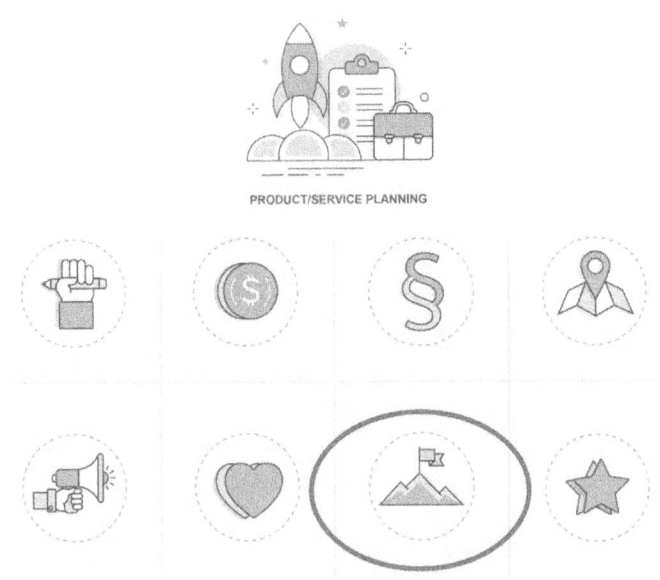

PRODUCT/SERVICE PLANNING

Field 9 - Improvement

IMPROVEMENT

The star stands for quality and awards. In order to achieve this, improvements are necessary. Therefore the star in the matrix stands for improvements.

Products and services are subject to a continuous improvement process. Functionalities, a used material or processes can be optimized. This can result in so-called product relaunches (a product is changed, improved again on the market). [3]If this is not the case, improvements can at least lead to savings that can improve the company's position. Missing technical innovations can mean the end for a company.

There is a possibility that the search for ways to improve the existing product or service may result in an innovation opportunity in the form of a new product or service.

Should an innovation arises in the course of this field, which could lead to a new product or a new service, the matrix can be run through again (for the new, innovative product).

The position was chosen because each product and each service need to be adapted over time. Improvements can even lead to an innovation.

---

[3] Cf. Pepels (2013): 394.

3 <u>The description of the matrix fields</u>

The following chapters now cover all main fields and their sub-fields.

3.1 Field 1 - Product Planning / Service Planning

1.2 Description of the product/service

PRODUCT/SERVICE PLANNING

I.   Description of the product/service

This subfield should be worded in such a way that an uninvolved third party can understand what the product/service is about and what the benefit to the customer of that product/service is.

Questions about the description of the product/service are for example:

- What is the idea?

This is about describing the product/service.

- How can the benefit be best described?

The benefit is product/service related. The benefit of a product/service is always to solve a "problem" of the customer.

Does the idea solve a problem? If so, which one? This is about the pure function that comes about through the product/service.

- Are there similar products/services?

If a product/service does not yet exist in the form in which it is to be offered, similar articles can help to explain the "innovation".

- Does the design play a role?

If design is an important factor, it can be described here.

- Are there "special" stakeholders?

If participants in production play an important factor, they can be described here (e.g. Disabled people, craftsmanship by regional artists, parents' initiative, etc.).

- Does the location play a special role?

In the service sector, the location usually plays a greater role than in manufacturing companies and should be communicated here.

- What is the technical state of the industry?

Can the product be manufactured with known machines? Can the service be provided by the current state of the art?

Under this point, details such as material and production method can also be given.

- Is there any additional benefit?

The additional benefit is a further advantage from the customer's point of view. This can result from image, price, design, special processes, etc. [4]

II.   Is there already such a product/service?

This question provides an initial rough answer to the follow-up question:

Who are the market participants for the product/service?

The market refers to the meeting of suppliers and consumers. Market participants are all suppliers (competitors) and consumers (customers) who appear on the emerging market.

---

[4] Cf. Weis 2013: 126.

If such a product or service already exists and the existing one is very similar (also in terms of availability), one should think about the meaningfulness.

A trading company should also answer the above questions. The reason for this is that the Personal product, even if it is bought, must be known. It must be known, which use it brings, which problem it solves and if necessary, how it is manufactured.

III.   Comparison of benefits

The benefits can also be compared directly with similar, already existing products/services. Here any factors can be named which represent the benefit for the customer. The figure (ABB 16) is a general example. Individually adapted, this benefit graph can quickly show essential factors and a real benefit. This quickly shows whether the product/service really brings a benefit.

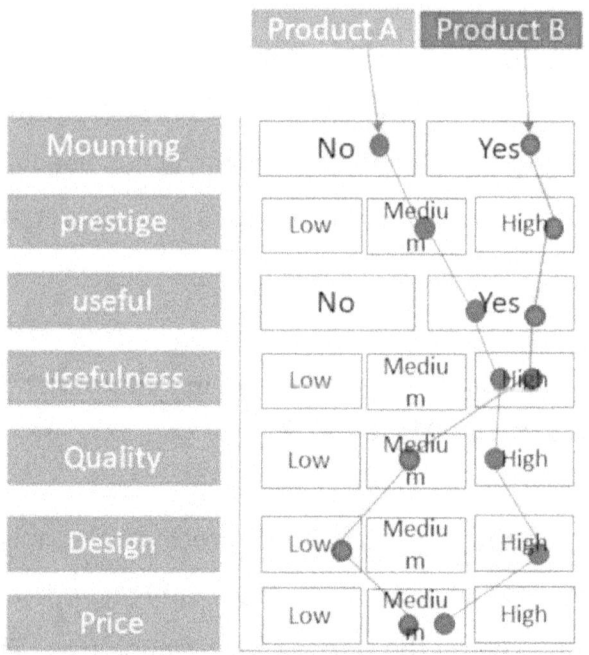

Figure 16 – Comparison of benefits

1.3 The cost of the product/service

PRODUCT/SERVICE PLANNING

This field is basically about dealing with everything that causes costs for the product/service. To do this, products/services must be broken down into their individual parts and these individual parts must then be quantified in monetary terms.

I.   Cost of the product/service

In the following, it is examined whether the product/service is financially feasible.

 # For manufacturing companies

It could make sense to make a prototype upstream. A prototype shows whether the "idea" can be implemented and whether special tools need to be developed for production. A prototype is also suitable for feedback, as mentioned in Field 1.9.

How much does Personal production (make) cost; how much does third-party production (buy) of the product cost?

When manufacturing a product, yourself, there are always three different cost areas involved.

1. Variable costs

2. Fixed costs

3. General costs

Example:

Variable costs are, for example, material costs that arise in the production of a certain product and can therefore be easily assigned to a product.

Fixed costs are, for example, costs for a machine that is required for production. This machine can / should then be calculated as a percentage of the respective product. Fixed costs also arise when nothing is produced.

The General costs result, for example, from the costs of sales, personnel, logistics, etc. It is not always easy to assign all costs 100 percent of the individual areas. For example, it is possible to allocate products according to the required production time, with a percentage surcharge on the general costs.

The US American Michael E. Porter identifies various cost factors in a company through his "value chain" (ABB19). Through this value chain, costs can be distributed in order to think about all factors. From the field "Processing (Operation/Production)" in ABB 17, the variable costs (e.g. Material) and, if applicable, the fixed costs (e.g. Machines) can be derived. Likewise, costs arise among other things for the purchase (by time) in the Field procurement. With startups, the point of exact cost distribution is often neglected. However, when a company grows, costs must be correctly analyzed and then distributed. [5]

---

[5] Cf. Finkreißen (1999): 42.

Porter´s Value Chain

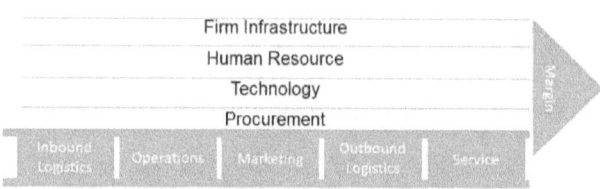

Figure 17 – Value chain according to Porter

Exemplary questions to determine and plan cost factors for your Personal production:

- Which machines are needed? (Fixed costs)
  - How much additional space do possible new machines need? (Fixed costs by renting/purchase/provision of space)
  - Which materials are to be procured and is this possible? (Variable costs)
  - What other fixed costs and what other variable costs does the production have?

In order to answer these questions, the product must be understood. The product must be planned and dismantled into all individual parts. This is the only way to identify all costs.

Individual processes can also be outsourced. Thus, mixed calculations of in-house and external production are also possible or can result.

II.   Task analysis of work processes

The task analysis is about analyzing tasks/processes. The analysis makes subtasks visible. Individual tasks can be derived from the subtasks.

Basically, the task analysis follows the didactic principle, "from general to detailed". The task analysis is therefore also important for the formation of organizational units, as it creates an initial assignment.

- A main task is defined (general).
- Subtasks are defined which approach the tasks in more detail.
- Depending on the complexity of the company, sub-tasks can be divided into individual tasks.

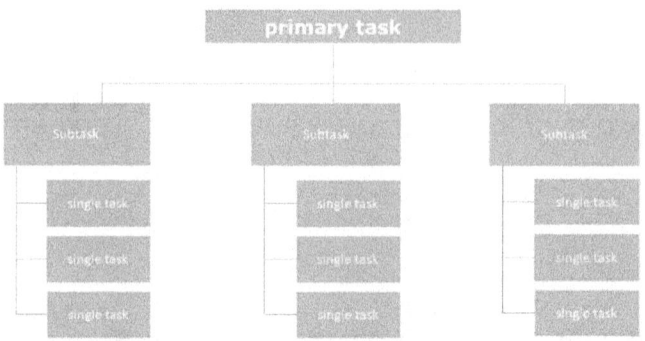

Figure 18 – Task analysis and task synthesis

In a manufacturing industry, for example, this could look like this:

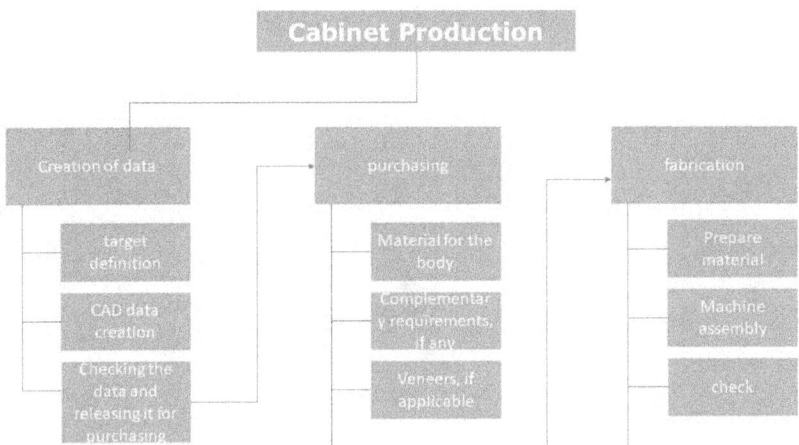

It should always be noted that work may influence each other. Good planning therefore indicates upstream and downstream tasks.

Example for marketing in a company (e.g. Also, as a service for customers):

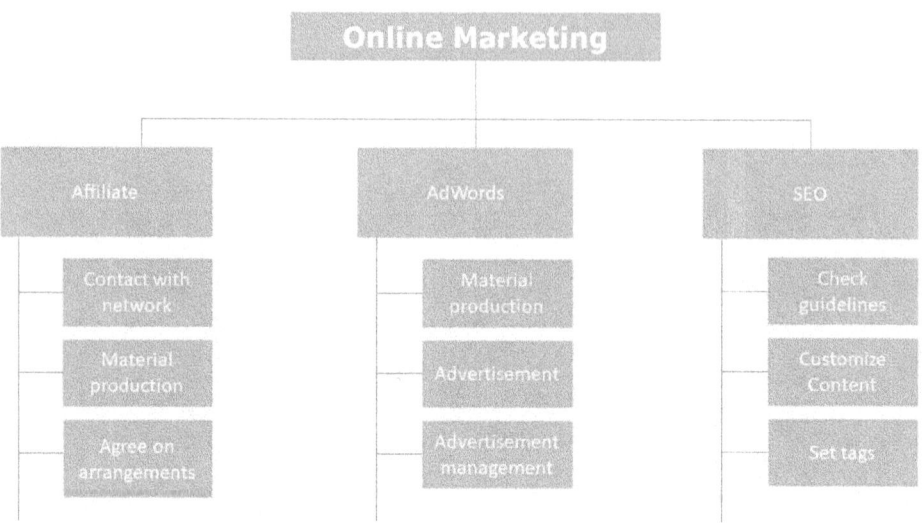

A detailed inventory is also important here - which of the production factors (e.g. Usable space, machines, manpower, materials, knowledge, etc.) are given.

By analyzing/dividing a product into individual tasks, all "sub-areas" can be quantified with costs. These can be added together and result in the total costs of the product.

By naming existing production factors, you can then name the other things you need. Thus, the basic module for ordering / procurement is put.

a) Make or Buy?

In the case of manufacturing industries, the question inevitably arises as to whether they should manufacture themselves (make) or whether they should produce externally (buy). The most important decision factors are costs and know-how. In the case of external production, the production processes are not "learnt" within the company; they are "outsourced". No new knowledge is created in the company.

Calculation for in-house production (make)

Material + production costs + other costs = Personal production

Production costs include not only the machines (machine hour rate), premises (rent, property taxes, credit rates, etc.) and ancillary costs, but also the personnel.

- What does it cost if personnel are needed for in-house production?
- What does it cost to have personnel if the logistics are taken over by the company itself? Is it worthwhile to use an external warehouse for small quantities, or can logistics be taken over in your Personal company without any problems?

- Gross wage + ancillary wage costs + any other charges + what else is to be observed for personnel (e.g. Additional vehicles)

Calculation for external production (buy)

Purchase price + costs for the purchase (e.g. Branding, transport, Din tests, etc.) = external production

To Make or Buy, customs duties and taxes may have to be added together (e.g. Import tax).

Which variant offers more advantages?

When deciding to make or buy, advantages and disadvantages have to be weighed. It is also important to consider all costs. Unexpected costs usually affect the entire company. An exact analysis of both procedures is therefore indispensable.

b) Changes due to larger output quantities

Is it possibly possible to produce more cheaply through larger investments?

How does the production quantity behave when production increases, e.g. when production increases?

- 25 %

- 50 %

- 75 %

- 100 %?

Industry experience can be used to this end. In business administration, the "experience curve" as seen in ABB 21 can also be found in this context. It states that, as a rule, doubling the output quantity (i.e. Doubling the quantity produced) reduces unit costs by between 20% and 30%. [6] Of course, this does not go to infinity, since costs still exist even in the largest output quantity.

This "theory" is derived from practice. A logical reason would be that series production is always more economical than individual production. If work is divided sensibly, savings can be made. The prerequisite for manufacturing in series (i.e. Larger quantities) lies in the possibility of being able to produce quantities at all.

---

[6] Cf. Heinen (2013): 666.

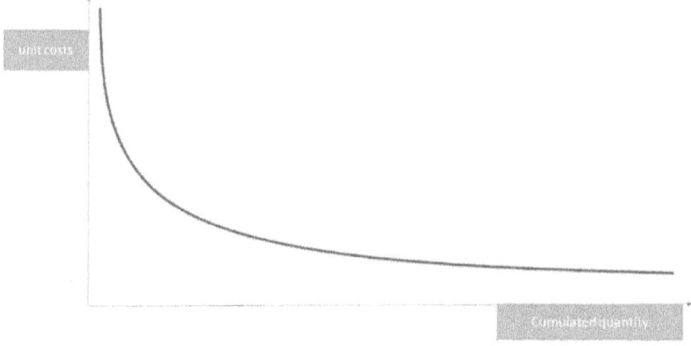

Figure 21 – Erfahrungskurve

c) Internal or external bearings

- In the case of in-house and external production, internal bearings can also be added. In-house warehouses can offer an advantage, as control is always possible. In-house warehouses can be positive or negative for logistics. Alternatives can be compared here. An important factor here is the aspect of whether space is available or not. New buildings must be planned carefully and on a long-term basis.

- In addition to our Personal warehouse, there are various external warehouses or fulfillment centers that take care of everything to do with logistics.

- For a calculation, different prices for transport to the customer may also have to be inquired here.

(a) Fulfillment, distribution centers

- The prices generally depend on the space taken plus a handling flat rate. Especially when companies want to expand abroad, foreign fulfillment centers can be an important partner. Fulfillment stands for all activities which are necessary after the purchase - the way of the product to the customer. It can also include invoicing and dunning.

(b) Factors influencing the costs of internal or external warehouses

- How high are the transport costs to your Personal location, an outsourced interim storage facility or fulfillment center?

- How does the choice of suppliers affect transport costs? (Comparisons of the individual providers)

- How high are the costs for your Personal warehouse?

 **For service companies**

When would it make sense to accept orders, when would it not?

Possible questions to analyze the sense of the order acceptance:

- Which production factors are given (e.g. Manpower, machines)?
- Is the knowledge for the implementation of planned tasks available to the employees?
- Is there enough time for the performance of the service?
- What does it cost if the work is done by the employees themselves (as far as possible)?
- (Determination of opportunity costs = lost money such as wages etc./own expenses, e.g. insurance, cost of living, taxes, membership fees etc.)
- Which tools/machines required to carry out the service? Also, here it is important to analyze the service completely in order to know what is needed.

The costs listed here show fixed costs. Fixed costs are costs that also arise without a service being provided. Variable costs for this example are e.g. the working time per hour, gasoline for vehicles and e.g. the chain saw, etc.

- What does it cost if personnel are needed to provide the service?
- Personnel + ancillary wage costs + any other levies + what else needs to be taken into account for personnel (e.g. Additional vehicles)
- What do comparable products / services of the competition cost? For this, it is necessary to find out who the competitors are.
- What are the possible transport costs to the customers?
- If the service is about producing as a service - contract manufacturing (e.g. CNC parts manufacturing for external companies as a service) can or must be included in the calculation of various factors that affect manufacturing industries.

III.   Further general points for manufacturing companies and service providers

- Are possible investments worthwhile (e.g. To win customers permanently)? If so, can this be secured by contracts? Is it possible to win new customers through this?)
- Here, too, it is important to analyze and know all the factors associated with an investment. The desired service must be thoughtfully disassembled.
- Does the product/service fit into the "time"? Is the economic phase suitable for the product? If wage rates, unemployment figures and economic growth fall, this can have a negative effect on the demand for "prestige" products. Conversely, this means that the demand for "prestige" products can be negative: If the economy booms, more luxury goods can be sold.

IV. Customer service costs

What does a possible customer service, warranty (defect rights) and guarantee cost?

A customer service / complaint management, which must be accessible, can defuse conflicts with customers and be an additional decision-making factor for the company by the customer - regardless of whether a company has one or ten products on the market and regardless of whether it is a service or trading company. The customer must always be the center of attention and taken seriously.

How much does possible returns cost?

Reserves should be planned for returns. It therefore makes sense to consider income only after the revocation period.

 **For trading companies**

A trading company must also ask itself the question of order picking (compiling goods and packaging them, if necessary) and weigh up whether in-house or third-party order picking is more suitable.

In the case of in-house order picking, various elements that can also be found in manufacturing companies (such as machines, halls, etc.) must be taken into account. An example of a "platform" for the search of service providers for order picking can be found in Field 1.5.

1.4 Legal aspects around the product/service

PRODUCT/SERVICE PLANNING

I. Trademarks, licenses, design protection & Co.

There are different ways to legally protect products and services. These include patents, design protection, and brand names. The legal framework is country-specific throughout the matrix and is only dealt with in very general terms here. Individual countries may have different regulations/laws which must always be observed.

Examples:

Does the product need

- a patent?
- a utility model? (Is, for example possible in Germany)
- Is it possible that patents of third parties are infringed? This should be checked by your Personal searches or preferably search by a lawyer.
- Does the product need a brand name? A service can also receive a trademark name. The fact that this is applied in practice can be seen from the fact that there are classes for services in the Nice Classification, which forms the basis of the classes in the trademark application. In the Nice Classification, services include classes 35-45.
- A strategy can be pursued with trademarks. The primary objective of the brand strategy is to increase the brand value through an "excellent" brand, which alone can justify a higher price.
- Does the service need its Personal name?
- Do products or services need a slogan?
- Does the product/service need a domain or is a general company website sufficient?
- Do already used brand names, slogans, domain names possibly violate the rights of other trademark owners/companies? Here, too, a search is indispensable in order to answer this question. In case of doubt, legal advice is always recommended.

- In spite of many things to consider with brand names, this can be of great importance for a company. Customers can find the product/service by name. In addition, the name builds a brand that can gain value separately.
- Is design protection required (e.g. For the logo/product)? This can be applied for at the DPMA (German Patent and Trademark Office) if you have your Personal design.
- Do Personal designs violate the design protection of others?
- Can images from the Internet be used (royalty-free) or have royalties been paid?

It makes sense to document rights to images, logos, etc. An example of this are files with which the logo was created or, for example, the invoice for the logo from the creator. It can also be useful to save images with a screenshot if they have been downloaded via free platforms.

II. Product liability

Product liability deals with the question:

What happens if someone gets injured/damaged in my goods/services?

In Germany, for example, product liability is regulated by the Product Liability Act (Product Liability Act/ProdHaftG). According to § 1 ProdHaftG, product liability occurs if someone is injured or killed by the product and if objects are damaged. Despite the most different legislations worldwide this legal point is almost always very important.

Are DIN standards to be observed?

- What about product liability? (The legal product liability applicable in some countries is intended to protect the consumer from dangers.)
- Is there an additional contractual product liability?
- What about liability for damages (including services)?
- What do contracts with possible manufacturing partners, distribution partners or customers have to contain?
- What is the best way to protect the product/service against legal action?
- Can legal ambiguities be researched precisely or is it useful to have a lawyer conduct a research?

III.   Legal influence on a product/service

The most important legal prerequisite is to examine whether the product/service may be offered in accordance with legal regulations. (Country-specific deviations reserved)

Examples:

- Medical Products
- Building regulations of municipalities (e.g. For architecture / building trade)
- When must the company be registered in order to work on the product/service? (Observe country-specific legislation)
- Is the product legally and politically feasible?

In case of doubt, legal advice is urgently recommended!

Some platforms/locations for the search of trademarks & Co. can be found under 4.5.

1.5 Purchasing/manufacturing locations for the product/service

PRODUCT/SERVICE PLANNING

I.   Providers/platforms

The word "place" also stands for supplier, as the supplier is a place where the goods are purchased.

Here it is a matter of finding the most suitable suppliers for the necessary purchase of the company. It is also necessary to examine the possible effects that a chosen location of suppliers can have.

Examples:

- Where can I get important tools for providing my service?

- Where can I have the product produced?

If the product is created by yourself:

- Where do I get the material from?
- Where do I get the machines from?
- Are there platforms for used machines?

Example:

- o http://www.gebrauchtmaschinen-kaufen.com/
- o https://www.maschinensucher.de/
- o https://www.plotterboerse.com

II. Advantages and effects of individual suppliers

What advantages does a certain supplier offer for purchasing?

Examples:

- Cheap?
- Warranty/guarantee?
- Customer service?
- High quality?
- Assumption of product liability?

What advantages (and disadvantages) does worldwide purchasing bring for "make" (materials) but also for "buy" (the complete product, or a partial product)?

What effect do the selected suppliers or production partners have on the company?

Examples:

- Duties
- unauditable quality
- Higher transport costs

Even if different platforms (suppliers) can make a financial difference, a certain advantage can outweigh it (e.g. Product liability in case of takeover by an externally producing industry, long warranty on company tools, etc.).

III. Provider for "make or buy

Here you will find a list of exemplary platforms where you can find suppliers for the production of products, partial production but also order picking and logistics services.

Examples:

- Who-supplies-what: https://www.wlw.de/de/firmen/kommissionierung-dienstleistung. / Direct link to suppliers who commission www.wlw.de

- Alibaba: www.Alibaba.com Here, too, products can be produced to customer specifications on request. In the meantime, companies from (almost) all over the world are represented on Alibaba.

- Picking, packing, gluing, or complete manufacturing, etc. - the workshops for disabled people WfbM offer a variety of possibilities. On the platform: https://www.werkstaetten-im-netz.de/ orders can be written out or also be selected and written down after suppliers on the basis of their descriptions.

- JVA's - many German prisons have workshops for different industries, which likewise take over various services for external companies. These are easy to find via the Google search.

IV.   Use value analysis

The utility analysis can be created to more quantify the decision making process for vendor selection. The utility analysis works with any criteria and the weighting of these. The utility value analysis also deals with the choice of alternatives. The total weighting of the individual criteria must be 100%.

In the comparison of the alternatives, a score (e.g. From 1-10) can also be awarded in the course of this.

The number of points awarded at the end can then be multiplied by the weighting. The highest overall result is thus the winner of the utility analysis.

In the example, the utility analysis is used for two coffee suppliers for a coffee project.

There are two possible partners for purchasing the coffee beans.

Criterion	Weight (self-cho-sen)	Part-ner 1	Points for Partner 1	Part-ner 2	Points for Partner 2
Delivery relia-bility	15%	9	15x9=135	5	15x5=75
Quality	40%	10	40x10=400	9	40x9=360
Delivery period	10%	7	10x7=70	7	10x7=70
Price	35%	5	35x5=175	9	35x9=315
	100%		780		820

According to the Personal established weighting, the benefit value analysis shows an advantage of partner 2 (820 points for partner 2; 780 points for partner 1).

1.6 Advertising slogan and packaging design for the product/service

PRODUCT/SERVICE PLANNING

I.   Advertising message/slogan

The advertising messages should communicate the clear advantage of the product/service and encourage purchase.

Again, as described in 6.4, it is important to respect the legal framework. It is country-specific to look at what is permitted - for example, in Germany according to the law against unfair competition, etc. - and to take a closer look at the legal framework.

The advertising statements should be adapted to the collo-quial language of the target group.

Creative messages help to stand out from the competition. However, creativity should not be so abstract that it cannot be understood.

The advertising message is the link between the customer and the product/service.

On the basis of the advertising message, the customer decides whether it is possible for him to think about, test or buy the product/service.

If there is no demand for the product/service yet, the right communication can generate demand.

II.   Graphic works

Define which graphic work is required for the product/service.

Examples of graphic work:

- Design of product and service logos, brand names and slogans (font, color, size,…)

- Development adapted to the design guidelines of the entire company if necessary (corporate design)
- Personal website for the product/service

This point falls under the category of graphic work, as there are various CMS systems where websites do not require any programming work and only graphic adaptations are necessary.

Examples:

Jimdo - www.jimdo.de

WIX - www.wix.com

WordPress - www.themeforest.com; https://www.template-monster.com/de/

Prestashop - https://www.templatemonster.com/de/

With Wordpress, Prestashop and other similar systems, hosting (providing web space) is separate, unlike Jimdo and WIX.

Some hosting partners install the "basic module" of Wordpress, etc. on customer request. The platforms mentioned above (Themeforest and Template Monster) can then be used to adapt the "basic template". WordPress and Prestashop require a lot more effort than Jimdo and WIX, but can make sense with more professional wishes.

III.   Design of packaging:

The general functions of packaging that should be considered are:

- Protective function of the product
- Dimension function
- Advertising through packaging [7]
- Carriers of information about handling etc.
- Possible reusability of the packaging
- Types of packaging are, for example:
- Gift packaging (as an additional option or from the outset as planned sales packaging for customers who plan to give away the goods)
- Transport packaging (packaging advantageous for logistics)
- Sales packaging (how customers find the goods in supermarkets, for example)
- Outer packaging (offer a second layer as protective packaging)

---

[7] Cf. Pepels 2017: 21.

A basic distinction is made between disposable and reusable packaging. [8]Nowadays, the possible composability of the packaging can also be important.

_____

[8] Cf. Otto (2008): 3.

1.7 Target group for the product/service

PRODUCT/SERVICE PLANNING

I.   Target group

The target group of a company refers to a defined group of people who come into question as potential customers. The more precise the definition of the target group, the better the entire company can be aligned with it.

A precise definition of the target group can be divided into demographic, socio-ecological and psychographic characteristics.

Demographic (descriptive) and socioeconomic characteristics (living conditions) are mostly measurable characteristics, e.g.:

68

- Age
- Sex
- Region
- Incomes
- Marital status
- Occupation
- Education

Furthermore, psychographic features that are difficult to measure or read, such as

- Desires
- Opinions
- Motivation
- Purchasing behavior
- Customer reaction to prices and price changes

II.   Size of the target group

If the assumed size of the target group differs greatly, there may be too few customers for the product and all invoices may fail. Likewise, with a much larger target group, there must be the possibility of producing faster.

The target group size is also important for the business plan.

The target group size can, for example, be researched on the Internet.

(E.g. Search engines, business registrations 2018, etc.).

The definition of the target group is the basis for market segmentation.

The aim of market segmentation is to gain competitive advantages.

III. Knowing the target group and knowing the market

Knowing the target group and the relevant competition are the two basic criteria for the success of a company.

This results in the following possibilities, among others:

- Define the overall market and determine the relevant sub-markets
- By "knowing" the customers (target group) you can respond more to their needs

- By knowing the relevant market (basis for the definition of the target group) one knows competing products and can accordingly take measures against new launches (e.g. By also introducing new products).
- Determine and improve one's Personal position (together with possible positioning tools)
- Be able to make forecasts about future developments
- Be able to use marketing instruments (4P/7P) in a more targeted way

From these possibilities follows:

- Lower scattering losses
- Save resources through optimization
- Increase of turnover and profit et.

1.8 Goals with the product/service

PRODUCT/SERVICE PLANNING

I. Target definition with the product/service

It is important to become aware of one's Personal goals.

Exemplary goals for founders:

- Solve a problem
- Be financially independent. Is financial independence achieved through the product/service or is it possible in principle?
- Earn more money than before

- Give other people a job
- Helping people
- Be the boss of one's own

A product should always bring a real benefit. [9] Of course, there are examples of products or services that have not brought any real benefit and are still successful, but this should not be a motivation.

If a product or service brings real added value to the customer, then an important basic building block for the future has been laid.

Modern marketing theories say that the question of why is of great importance for the success of a product or service.

Thus the question:

Why do we bring this product/service onto the market?

The answer to the question "Why" can be communicated to customers (tip: Start with Why: How Great Leaders Inspire Everyone to Take Action by Simon Sinek)

---

[9] Cf. Bleiber (2011): 56.

1.9 Product/service improvements

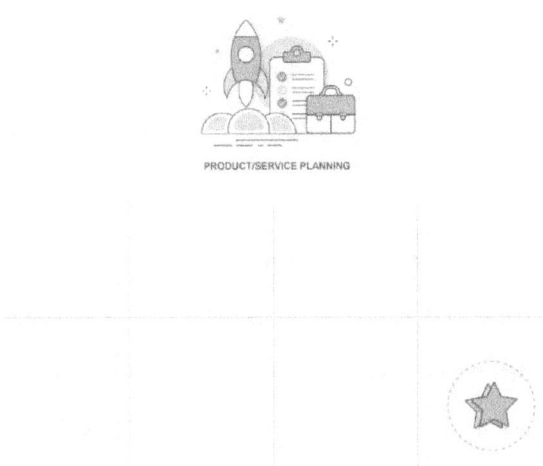

PRODUCT/SERVICE PLANNING

I. Improvement through feedback

The word product blindness usually refers to a condition in which an entrepreneur or a team no longer recognizes mistakes because they have lost their objective view of them. One loses often the overview, if one was occupied for a long time with a certain topic (product/service).

Even if you yourself are convinced that the planned product/service could not be improved any more, external feedback providers can be helpful to optimize/improve the product/service.

Feedback providers can be involved either from the beginning, during the manufacturing process, or "at the end" of the manufacturing process.

Especially for startups a culture of "one hand washes the other" could develop - that means "I give you feedback and you give me".

Friends, acquaintances and relatives are usually only suitable for feedback/questionnaires to a very limited extent, since these are usually biased. As an alternative to other startups, professional market research companies can be commissioned with product testing. Some companies offer special prices for startups.

Even if costs arise from this sub-item, one should not shy away from them. It has to be considered that the earlier you get professional feedback, that the product/service can be changed/optimized and that you take this into account, you save more than if you discover this change/optimization later and have it done. If a product or service is already on the market, changes/optimizations cost many times more than this would be the case if changes were already made in the planning phase.

II.   Unique selling point (USP)

USP = Unique selling proposition = unique selling proposition = the characteristic/s in which a product/service differs from products/services of other competitors. [10]

Other products, thus designate products of the competition. The USP has been always about a competitive advantage. This can be defined, among other things, as in the utility graphic in 1.2. The benefit was defined in Field 1.2, a defined advantage can thus be derived 1:1 and, if necessary, communicated.

---

[10] Cf. Fleing, Evers (2008): 35.

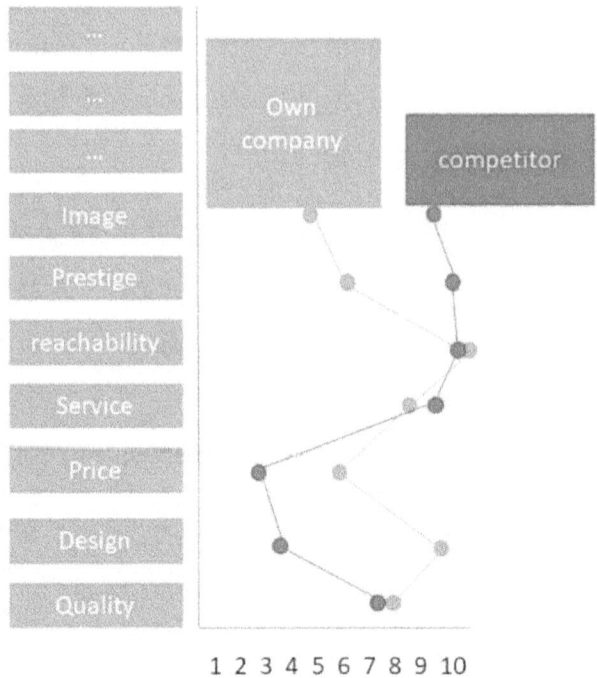

Figure 22 – Defining the USP

The USP clarifies the answer to the question: What is special about the product/service in contrast to existing products/services? Which competitive advantage is recognizable? [11]

---

[11] Cf. Poth, Pradel, S. Poth 2011: 342.

Examples of questions about the USP:

- What makes the product/service special?
- What sets it apart from the competition?
- What additional benefits does it offer? (Added benefit, since every product or service should always have a benefit.)
- What does the unique selling proposition cost?
- What are the costs of the USP?

Examples of USPs across all industries compared to the competition:

- Excellent location
- Special design
- Particular innovation
- Special, outstanding quality
- Nice, friendly staff throughout
- Special guarantees
- Special customer service
- Special properties of the material
- Special properties during production
- Particularly fair

A USP helps to answer the question:

Why should the customer buy exactly this product or use exactly this service?

The USP is, as described in 1.6, to communicate further to the customer as a means of persuasion or to provide the customer with further positive facts relevant for decision making.

III.   Improving the product/service in the future

This is about collecting ideas for improving the product/service in the future.

Example of improvement:

- Are there already ideas for innovations for the future of the product/service?

Innovations refer to products that are absolutely or relatively new on the market. Innovation can come about through technology and/or new ideas.[12] It is only a product innovation if it is also marketable. Innovations can also be new products/services which deviate from the actual product/service and which

---

[12] Cf. Thudium (2015): 156.

may be suitable for certain niches. An innovation does not necessarily have to affect the entire previous target group.

- Are there any ideas for improvement in terms of design?

Design means shaping. In addition to the design / shaping that is important for the technical aspect, attention should also be paid to aesthetics.

- Are there any ideas for improving quality?

Quality means meeting a set requirement. Quality is one of the most important criteria for purchasing decisions. There are certifications e.g. by DIN EN ISO 9000 ff. A lack of quality can result in a recall and thus cause high and mostly avoidable costs for a company.

- Are there any ideas for product variations?

Variation means a technical or aesthetic change/improvement to the product. A well-known example of variation is the face-lifting of cars.

- Are there ideas for product differentiation?

Product differentiations refer to ideas that serve the same market and additionally offer the product in a modified form.

- Are there already ideas for expanding the product portfolio?
- Are there already ideas for optimizing the product portfolio?
- Are there already ideas for growth strategies?
- Are there any ideas for niches?

IV.   Definition of niches

A niche product/service is a product/service that fits into an empty and possibly undiscovered part of the market. A niche is a part of the overall market that is not yet overcrowded by competition. There is, so to speak, a gap into which a product or service can be easily placed. A niche can facilitate market entry and possibly lead to results more quickly.

An example of a niche:

Overall market	Niche
• Barbecue sauces	• 100% organic, regional barbecue sauces

A Personal analysis, whether a niche would be worthwhile, can be meaningful.

3.2 Field 2 - Strategic planning

STRATEGIC PLANNING

2.1 Production/performance strategy of the company

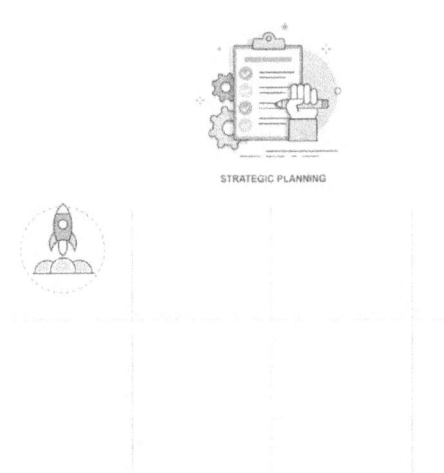

STRATEGIC PLANNING

I.   The strategies around the product

The strategies for manufacturing around the product/service must be defined.

This subfield is clearly more important or more interesting for producers/traders than for service providers, but also for service providers the question of working with subcontractors or the exclusive provision of services by their Personal personnel sometimes arises.

Of course, different strategies can be chosen for different products/services.

- Determine make or buy
- Determine whether internal or external bearings are to be used
- Defining the scope of the service policy (customer service, etc.)
- Defining the Service Performance Strategy
- What is the rationale behind the company's manufacturing/performance strategy?

    Example:

    - The main thing is "homemade" or produced internally?
    - as cheap as possible?
    - generate as many orders as possible?
    - Strategies can be derived from this "basic idea

2.3 Pricing strategy of the company

STRATEGIC PLANNING

I. Costs

Final costs must be defined in order to carry out further steps, such as the pricing strategy.

Examples

- List of the final purchase/production price per quantity and time, with a scale if necessary.
- List of total (planned) investment costs (depending on decisions such as "make or buy", internal or external storage, etc.)

II.   Prices

After this field, it should be clear how the company defines its Personal pricing strategy. In the following, different, frequently used models for the price strategy are named. Defining a pricing strategy means that a company must find a strategy that fits its Personal company. The advantage of such a definition is that subsequent products/services can be quickly provided with a sales price using the method defined here. This procedure not only offers the advantage that less time is spent on defining the price in the future, but also that future products/services or their sales can be better planned financially.

III. The best possible pricing strategy

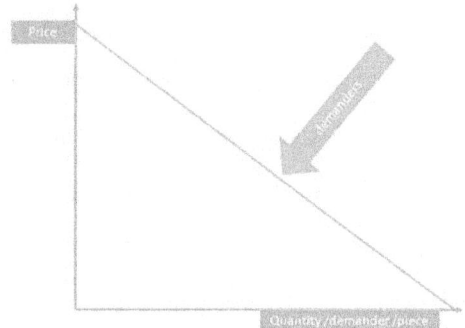

Figure 23 – Finding the strategic price

Ultimately, it's always about the customer. If the customer does not buy his Personal product, there is no turnover. Even the best products may not be sold, even if the price is justified. The price is in most cases an important influencing factor. The upper graph is an example of this. The lower the price, the higher the purchase. Of course, even with the best product at the best price, the purchase in quantity is limited at some point. Also a product/service may not be so favorable that a customer doubts its quality.

Older models, such as Porter's competitive strategies, assume (ABB 32 + 33) that uniqueness (almost) always costs more. This must be questioned in any case.

The most important thing in pricing is to determine the best possible price.

How can I determine such a price?

The answer to this question falls within the field of market research. Entire companies have specialized in this area. The methods of market research include observation and questioning. Thus, you can observe similar products and see in which price class they are particularly well distributed, or you can conduct surveys yourself or commission them.

With a systematic, meaningful survey you can determine the best possible price for your product/service. Surveys should be conducted in the places where the potential target group can be found. Also, an honest feedback from relatives, other startups, friends and acquaintances offers first clues. Here the bias (as mentioned in 1.9) has to be considered. Extremes in surveys can, but do not have to, be taken into account. It is more about a "healthy" mean, a value that the average would be willing to pay.

As an example, this can be determined graphically as follows:

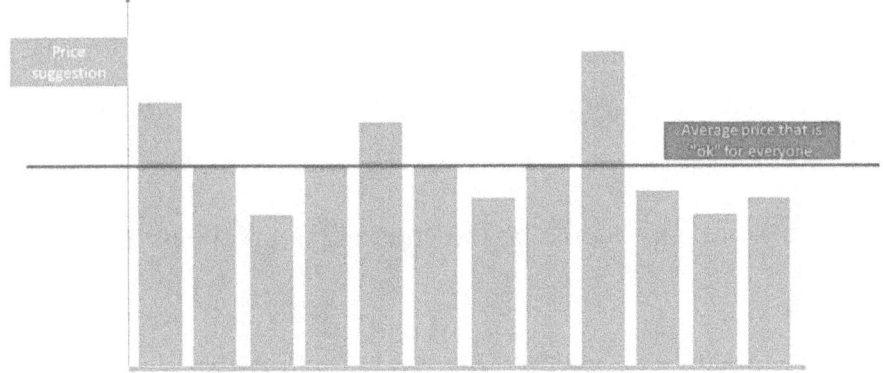

Figure 24 – the healthy mean value

Here, an excellent indicator is formed immediately as to whether the company can be implemented.

If the "researched" price is not realizable (e.g. Due to too high production costs and a correspondingly low margin), the meaningfulness of the enterprise must be examined.

a) Van Westendorp method

The Van Westendorp method is an effective method of determining price readiness for a product/service.

Four questions are presented to the respondents that relate to the price of the product/service.

1 Which price would be too high and would lead to the product/service not being purchased? (Curve 1)

2. What price would be expensive, but would not rule out the purchase decision? (Curve 2)

3. What price would be too cheap to doubt the quality? (Curve 3)

Four. What would be a good offer? (Curve 4)

The results are plotted on a graph and the four resulting curves show the acceptable price range.

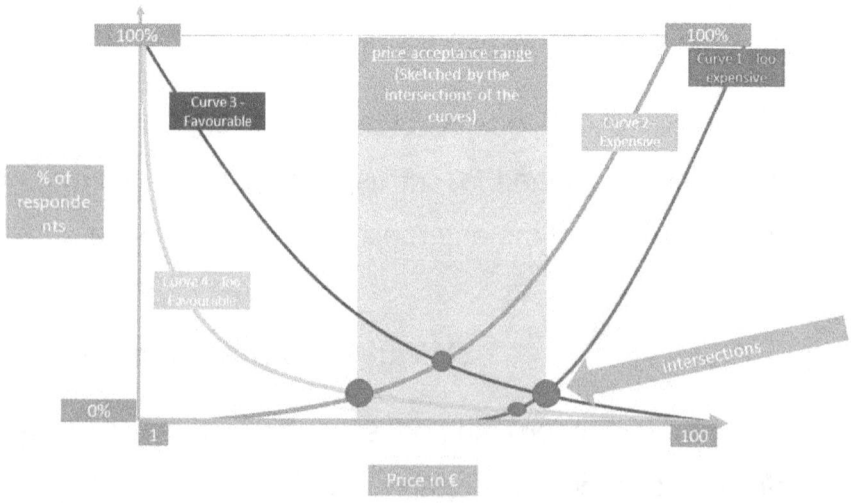

Figure 25 – Van Westendorp Method

As mentioned in 1.9, respondents interviewed by this method can represent other startups, relatives, friends and acquaintances, if their bias is taken into account. Likewise, respondents can be found via platforms such as eBay classifieds or other online marketplaces. Market research agencies (which can be commissioned for optimal pricing, if necessary) or the like carry out such surveys with panels. A panel refers to a group that corresponds to the target group definition.[13]

IV.   Optimization of the production price

If the willingness to pay is too low, it can be checked whether savings can be made in production.

Exemplary ideas to identify savings potential:

- Optimization by omitting certain, unnecessary parts/processes

---

[13] Cf. Vgl. https://www.appinio.com/de/preisanalyse-van-westendorp-methode (see:14. Mai 2019)

- Optimizing workflows (an excellent example of this can be found in the film "The Founder", when the Mc Donalds brothers optimize their workflow in their restaurant)
- Ask employees whether manufacturing processes can be changed
- Benchmarking to check whether processes can be improved (more about benchmarking in 6.9)
- Check whether an additional benefit can be generated in order to achieve a higher price. Here, too, the price of the new or modified product should be researched again, as already described.
- Examine whether further markets or niches could be opened up with little effort in order to produce/offer larger quantities and thereby reduce the costs for the individual product/service.
- At the end of this step some points should be established:
- Final offer/sale price
- Possible price differentiations (see below 2.3.IX Price differentiations)
- Possible conditions (discounts e.g. loans, installment payments or leasing?)

V. Further questions about the strategic price

Are your Personal prices competitive (whether service or product)?

If not:

- Is your Personal quality better?
- Does this product/service offer a much greater benefit than comparable products/services?
- Are the prices marketable?
- Can the price be accepted by the market?

VI. The market

The market is the place where buyer and seller meet. The market is about making an offer to solve a problem/need for which there is (potential) demand.

If there is no direct demand, this must be created for the respective product/service. Quote from Steve Jobs: "Get closer than ever to your customers. So close that you tell them what they need well before they realize it themselves. "From the point of view, this sentence means: "Be so close to the customer that you tell him what he needs before he realizes it himself."

The price usually plays an important role in buying decisions. For example, if the price is too high in comparison with similar products/services, the customer must have other advantages from the offer (USP - more in Field 1.9). These advantages must also be communicated. If the customers do not know anything about it, they will probably not be considered by the customers in the decision-making phase.

VII.   Pricing policy

The basis for price formation in business administration is called "price policy". The term price policy comes from marketing and reflects the attitude to want to participate as successfully as possible in market events.

Price policy is an important point of contact between companies and customers. Therefore, the price policy is to choose a price that is as attractive as possible for the customer (without valuing the amount).

VIII.   General price formation

Pricing is most often based on the 3K rule. The three "K" stand for the influencing factor costs, customers and competition.[14]

Costs arise from the consumption of goods and services in the respective production process.[15] BWL distinguishes between fixed, variable and general costs. The price, which is based on the cost of manufacture/performance, takes into account the variable costs incurred, portions of fixed and general costs (such as the usage area), and the planned profit. The reseller discount is deducted from the planned sales price.

In competitive pricing, the aim is to exploit a price advantage (price leadership) over the competition. However, there are considerable risks involved in going along financial lower limits only to bring a product onto the market or to keep it there. In order to consistently implement this "price leadership", competitors must be constantly monitored.

---

[14] Cf. Weis 2017: 159.

[15] Cf. Götze (2010): 27.

Customer-oriented pricing has the advantage that customers accept the price. Extensive market research is required to determine the perfect price from the customer's point of view (see e.g. 2.3.a)). An initial comparison of similar competing products and their prices in order to initially analyze a price usually paid by customers can also be found in price databases or online research.

A field of tension arises when the price is fathomed by the 3 Cs. The influence of the 3 K on each other must also be taken into account. For example, a pure cost price could practically eliminate demand if the customers' willingness to pay is virtually ignored.

IX.   Price differentiations

Price differentiation offers the advantage that the same products can be sold at different prices to different customer groups. To this end, the target overall market must be clearly distinguishable into at least two submarkets. Observations must be possible in a strictly differentiated manner in order to be able to assess submarkets separately. Price differentiation should always have a reason. [16]

There are various possibilities for segmentation. These are e.g.:

- Differentiation by region, e.g. domestic and foreign (also possible by different brand names)
- Differentiation through time, campaigns, beginner discounts, pre-order or seasonal prices
- Differentiation according to the quantity - e.g. a differentiation of the dealer conditions is possible depending on the quantity purchased.
- Differentiation according to use: private or commercial
- Differentiations according to scope: with additional options or only the "raw product"

---

[16] Cf. Hingston (2001): 36.

2.4 Strategy for the legal framework of the company

STRATEGIC PLANNING

I.   Own company/competition analysis

The company is the legal contact - country-specific deviations reserved.

One of the advantages of corporations can be their limited liability. Disadvantages are higher costs for registration (by a notary) and more extensive taxation.

As soon as a company is registered in the commercial register, an independent company name can be chosen. Certain institutions usually offer the service by checking the desired company name for the possibility of registration.

II.   Special forms of companies

Franchising

In franchising, a contract is concluded between the franchisor and the franchisee which regulates future cooperation. The cooperation is based on a generally functioning business, which can include goods and services. The franchisee uses all the franchisor's know-how, company names, etc. in return for one-off and regular payments. The advantage is that it is based on an experienced (and often already known) system, the disadvantage is the franchisee's limited room for maneuver.

Franchising is also a common form of cooperation in foreign trade.

With a franchise, the franchisee trades in his Personal account and on his Personal name - thus this is connected with his Personal registration of the company - but with a close contractual relationship.

III. Direct competitor

Who is the direct competitor? This question can be answered by "market research". Searches in the yellow pages or Google searches help to quickly identify competitors. The definition of competitors is about finding companies that offer the same service/products or offer products or services that would replace one's own.

Describe the competitor as precisely as possible:

- Company size
- Form of enterprise
- Portfolio
- Turnovers

a) Influences

Which groups/situations have the greatest influence on your Personal success or failure besides direct competition?

- Clients
- Suppliers
- Is the market entry of further companies imminent?
- Is there a risk of substitution products?
- How do my existing competitors behave?

Porter addresses this question with the industry structure analysis - also known as the five-forces model.

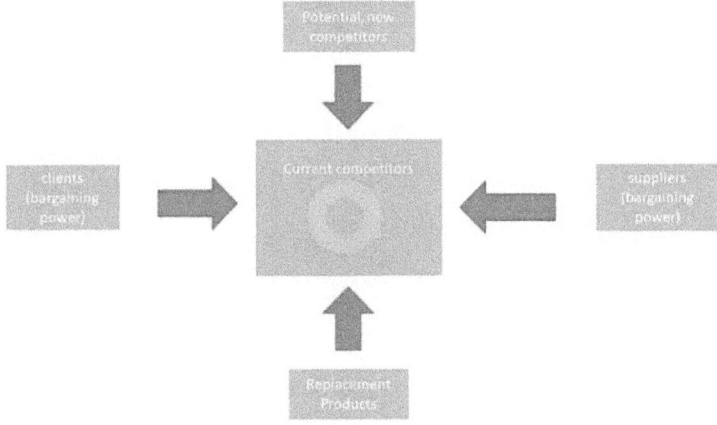

Figure 27 – 5 Forces model according to Porter

According to Porter, they therefore exist:

- Negotiating strength of customers (benefit/price/quality)
- Negotiating strength of suppliers
- The existing competition and its activities

- The power of new competitors entering the market with the same product, but also of
- Competitors supplying substitute products

These "5 forces" can strongly influence the Personal strategy and planning, since the situation on the market can change with these.[17] It is therefore important to always consider these factors in order to identify risks, but also to take advantage of possible opportunities. The use of the chances and neutralization of the risk results from the acceptance of the changes with the Personal strategy.

---

[17] Cf. Knop (2009): 58.

IV. SWOT analysis

Compare your Personal company with your competitors using a SWOT analysis.

The SWOT analysis is a widely used instrument and it is worth working with it. The SWOT analysis deals with internal strengths and weaknesses as well as external opportunities and risks.

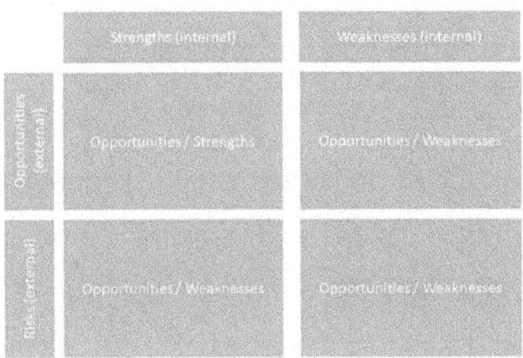

Figure 28 – SWOT Analysis

Opportunities and strengths" are entered in the first field. External factors (opportunities and risks) are external influencing factors. External" factors are usually the market (other companies and consumers) but also legal regulations such as laws or other regulations and technical developments. Strengths can be e.g. the Personal know-how, flexibility, flat decision ways, etc. Strategies can thus be derived from the analysis results of the fields. In the SWOT analysis, it makes sense to first describe the external factor. The internal factor (here strengths) can then be determined on this basis. If, however, you were to list all the strengths of the company here, this would go beyond the scope of this analysis. Of course, more than one external and one internal factor can be mentioned.

The field "Opportunities and Weaknesses" is about identifying opportunities (from outside) and describing one's Personal weaknesses (honestly). Opportunities can, if used correctly, transform weaknesses into strengths.

The field "Risks and Strengths" is about analyzing risks and comparing them with one's Personal strengths.

In the "Weaknesses and Risks" field, it is a matter of developing a strategy that neutralizes the risks and transforms the weaknesses as best as possible so that these two factors cannot cause any damage.

Especially in times when customers find a large range of products on the market, it is becoming increasingly important to eliminate even small weaknesses in order to prevent customers from changing supplier.

The SWOT analysis is often found in strategic marketing.

2.5 Positioning strategy

STRATEGIC PLANNING

I.   Positioning for the product/service

It is necessary to determine where the product/service should be placed on the market.

The "where" denotes a market or sub-market. In order to be able to describe a market, the target group - part of the target group are the customers - and the other providers must be known and described. [18]The target group definition and size come from 1.7.

---

[18] Cf. Stamminger (2008): 2.

The point of positioning is to be assigned to marketing.

The positioning can influence if necessary, the basic idea. If the positioning shows that the Personal product must exist on the existing market among innumerable suppliers, the product could be adapted or changed for another market.

The most frequent criteria for a positioning are price and quality / performance. [19]

The determination of price and quality, as well as a possible adjustment of the two criteria for the market entry, precede the positioning. Market entry is the point at which a company offers products or services and becomes visible to other suppliers and consumers.

A market entry can take place due to a new establishment. Offering new products to new markets is also a market entry.

---

[19] Cf. Hofbauer, Sangl (2017): 429.

II.   The positioning cross

A positioning cross, which is fed with data from drill down re-
porting, is suitable for defining or recognizing your Personal
position.

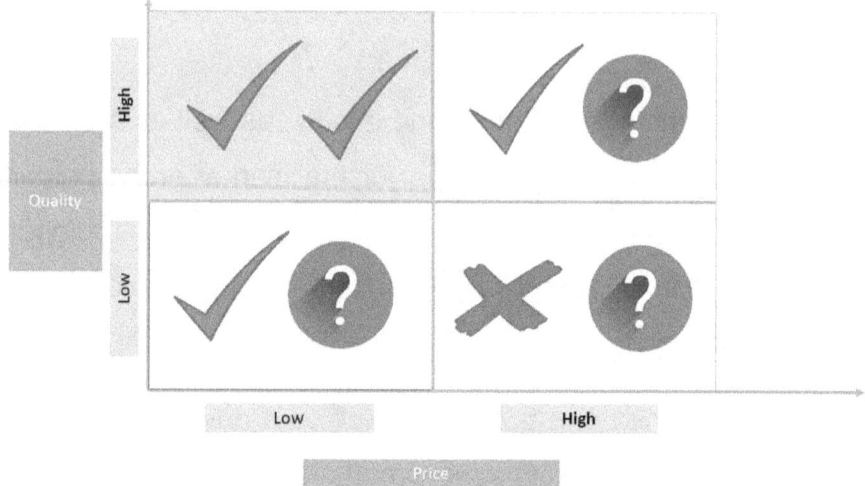

Figure 29 - positioning cross

The positioning cross does not necessarily have to have the
criteria quality and price, although these are probably the
most common in practice.

The positioning cross usually measures the price in comparison to similar products on the market. The instrument is intended for internal use and can influence decisions. The user

of the cross can therefore check himself and, if the result is negative, change or even cancel the company. A higher price and lower quality can also be sold if there is a strategy behind it. As a rule, this combination is of course bad. The positioning cross must therefore match the strategy.

III.   The competitive matrix

Michael E. Porter defines the positioning cross differently.

As described in Field 2.3, newer models (e.g: The Blue Ocean as strategy: How to create new markets where there is no competition (book)) no longer assumes that uniqueness has to cost more and more. The Porter model is described here for the sake of completeness. The basic idea that one must always differentiate oneself from other suppliers and that cost leadership is generally very good is also highly topical and extremely important for newer models. New models combine both strengths of differentiation. With traditional approaches, one advantage over the competition is enough.

With its matrix, Porter practically assumes that quality costs more and thus form the opposite side of an axis to costs. Both axle parts result in a strategic advantage. One part of the axis

- the quality part - provides the strategic advantage of quality leadership.

The other part of the axis - the cost advantage - provides the strategic advantage of cost leadership.

The other axis is the market.

The two axis parts of the market are divided into:

- Segment of the industry (submarket)
- The entire industry-wide market. [20]

The quality-price axis influences this axis, since the advantages mentioned above (quality and cost leadership) affect the entire or submarket.

---

[20] Cf. Intveen (2013): 128.

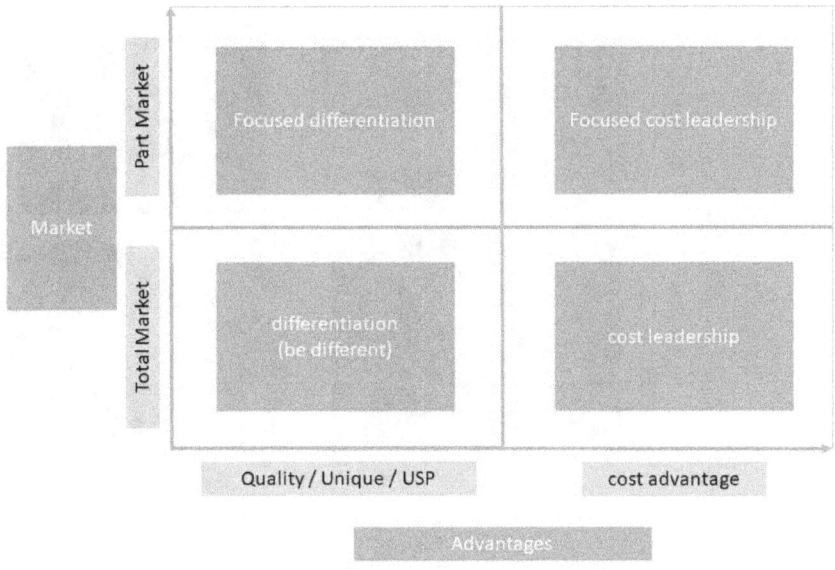

Figure 30 – Competition matrix empty [21]

The following positions cross shows real examples of the automotive industry:

[21] Cf. Vry (2017): 161

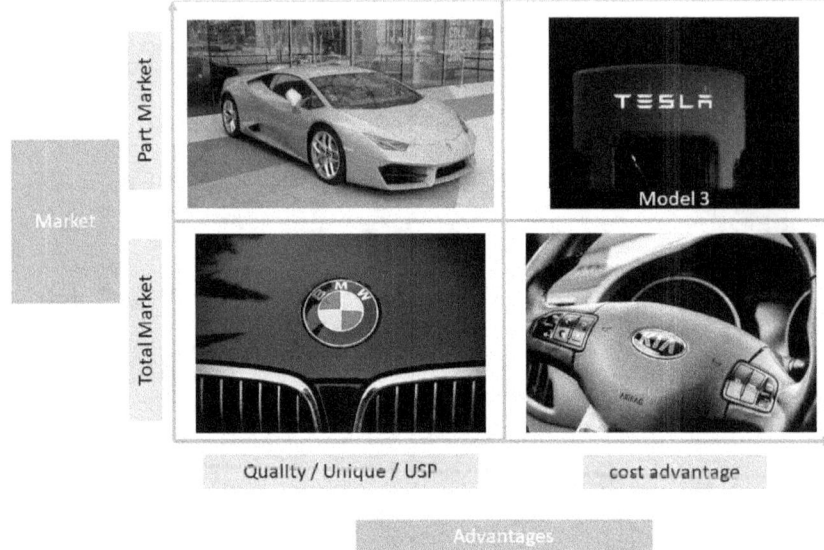

Figure 31 – Competition matrix passenger car

The advantage of a few or one segment (submarket) is that it can be reached or made known more quickly within the segment. The disadvantage is that other segments are not reached.

The disadvantage with many/all segments (entire market) is that it costs considerably more resources such as time and money to reach all. It requires well thought-out planning to reach and reach potential customers. The advantage of the overall market is the possibility of an increase in turnover, an expansion of potential customers. There is a great potential for growth.

Def. differentiation strategy: As a rule, always an important strategy to differentiate yourself or to be unique. Differentiation is about standing out from other providers, e.g. through quality or image.

Def. cost leadership strategy: Usually an important strategy to make the product/service affordable. The goal is to create an advantage through a lower price.

IV.   Points and locations of sale

Where should the product/service be marketed?

Where should the company be made visible?

The choice of sales platform has an influence on logistics. This must be taken into account when making the selection, as logistics costs (depending on the product) can entail a large (new) cost factor.

 **Producing companies**

Is direct or indirect sales chosen?

In direct sales, sales are made directly from the company to the customer.

Examples:

- (Self-used) sales platforms on the Internet, e.g. Amazon, Google Shopping, Ebay
- Personal shop
- Personal webshop
- Weekly markets/sales carts/crafts markets (market events offer a direct advertising effect without additional material solely through the presence)

With indirect sales, the products do not come directly to the customer, but via an intermediary.

Examples:

- Wholesale
- Retail
- Authorized dealer

- Sales intermediaries (these are legally independent companies independent of the manufacturer (except for specific contracts)).

 # Service companies

Where is the service best offered and presented?

Factors influencing decisions on the selection of locations: criteria can be transported and/or travel costs from the location to the customer or to a further processing platform.

Further selection factors can be the strength of the presence of competitors at a chosen location.

The number of customers at a location (regardless of whether it is virtual or real) is also decisive.

Examples:

- Personal website
- Print yellow pages (in Germany e.g. yellow pages)
- Online business directories
- Platforms for tenders for contracts (mostly online)

- Office/practice in the respective region (good, visible location can be of great advantage)

2.6 The advertising strategy

STRATEGIC PLANNING

I.   General advertising strategies

Various general advertising strategies can be found in the literature.

Examples:

Advertising strategy for the market launch: to become known, build image, generate turnover, communicate USP and uniqueness.

Expansion advertising: gaining market share, exploiting market opportunities, increasing turnover.

Reminder advertising: Reminder of the product/service to keep sales (or even the brand) stable.

Conservation advertising: Defending the market share through advertising. [22]

II.   Media/tools for advertising

Which media and tools should be used to make the company known? As an important decision factor the existing finances have to be taken into account. The costs for advertising or trying out different advertising strategies should not be underestimated, as these are often higher than planned, especially without experience.

It is advisable to stick to Henry Ford's quote:

"Who does not advertise, dies!

The planning of the finances for this part can be found in 3.6.

---

[22] Cf. Vry (2017): 455.

In this field, it must be said that there is usually a market launch advertising strategy. This (usually) means a considerable additional financial expense of advertising than with a permanent advertising strategy.

The permanent advertising strategy must also be planned and can, for example, be a modification of the market launch strategy.

Examples of media and tools:

 **Producing companies**

Wholesale:

- Advertising in flyers/catalogues of wholesale customers (usually possible via wholesalers)
- establish direct contact with wholesale customers

Retail trade:

- Contact the retailer directly and present products

- Offer of special cooperation (e.g. Through Personal shelves; display against extra payment; buying or renting POS positions (POS = Points-of-Sale) which increase sales because they are clearly visible).

Sales platforms on the Internet:

- Tags
- Keyword marketing
- SEO (search engine optimization)
- Content management
- Google's guidelines are followed to increase reach
- Banner advertising
- sponsored search ads
- Highlight articles / Rent positions
- positive ratings
- Verifications
- Linked articles from magazines, daily newspapers, blogs

Personal shop:

- Flyer/business cards/posters/banners (print) on advertising spaces
- Articles in regional newspapers/magazines (public relation) to draw attention to the company and or improve its reputation
- Advertisements in regional newspapers/magazines
- A website is also important for a retail shop. With Google searches, the shop can be found more quickly for the determination of opening times or a route description.

Sponsoring (donations against advertising / space for advertising)

A distinction is made here between:

- Sports sponsoring e.g. football clubs
- Cultural sponsoring e.g. museums
- Sociosponsoring e.g. social projects
- Eco sponsoring e.g. "x m2 rainforest preservation when buying our products".
- Programme sponsoring, e.g. before radio shows "sponsored by..".

- Sponsoring can also be carried out on a supra-regional basis, especially in the case of product placement. Product placement is e.g. product placements in films in order to unconsciously perceive the product. Product placement sounds expensive and complex, but it can also be a relatively inexpensive way of advertising small projects (depending on the project). One possibility is to make agreements with start-up film producers (which correspond to the target group). These can be found at Start Next or Kickstarter.

Personal webshop

- SEO
- Google AdWords
- Links from other, external advertisements such as Facebook, Twitter and Co.
- Compliance with guidelines, recommendations from Google
- Content management - (this question should be asked: What content must be communicated on the website?)
- Compliance with Google guidelines/recommendations (this improves the ranking)

- Enter company data such as opening hours, contact, etc. directly in Google
- Affiliate Platforms
- Another possibility for Personal webshops is advertising via affiliate platforms (more in 6.5), which offer among other things:
- fair commissions to the partners to get better positions
- Banner advertising
- Content
- Attractive advertising texts
- Blog article
- Coupon actions

 **For service companies**

Personal Website

- SEO

- Google AdWords

- Links from other, external advertising, e.g. Facebook, Twitter and Co.

- Content management

- Compliance with Google policies/recommendations

- Entering company data such as opening hours, contact, etc. directly on Google so that they can also be found via them

- Regional advertising
- In contrast to the own, not regionally limited online shop of a manufacturing industry, regional advertising has to be considered here. If this is not directly bookable or adjustable, keywords with place, city and/or region designation help.
- Print industry directories = buy/rent entries/premium entries, place advertisements
- Online business directories = buy/rent entries/premium entries, place advertising
- Platforms for tenders of contracts = evaluations, content management, images
- Office in the respective region = uses posters, advertising foils, showcases, signs, areas
- regional advertising = flyer/business cards/posters/banners (print) on advertising spaces
- Articles in regional newspapers/magazines
- Advertisements in regional newspapers/magazines
- Sponsoring (against advertising), e.g. football clubs, ..

III.   Graphic works

Which graphic works are necessary for the company?

Examples of graphic work:

- Design of company logo, company name, company slogan
- Design of business cards, invoices etc.
- Development if necessary, adapted to the design guidelines of the entire company (corporate design)
- Design of the company website (more information, see 1.6)

2.7 Strategy for personnel and target group

STRATEGIC PLANNING

I.   Strategy for employee recruitment

At this point, it is a question of determining how the Personal company is to be set up in terms of personnel.

 For business startups

For the initial situation, a profile, short profile of the founder, the employees and a description of the position(s) in the future company must be described.

Examples of the personal starting position of the founder:

- Marital status (can, but does not have to be interpreted as a sign of seriousness)
- Occupation
- Study
- Relevant prior knowledge (courses, personal experience)
- Professional background: What qualifies me, the founder/self-employed person?

II. Strategy for the selection of suitable employees

What qualifies employees or freelancers?

Who can be considered as future personnel?

III. Formation of organizational units

The organizational structure of an enterprise determines how individual areas are structured. In the organization, positions (the smallest units in the organization) and instances are defined. Also the hierarchy of the enterprise is decided in the organizational structure.

The organizational structure of a company has a great influence on the success of the company and makes a major contribution to effectiveness and efficiency.

a) Task synthesis and position

Following the task analysis (1.3), the task synthesis summarizes individual subtasks.

Through the systematic grouping of subtasks, jobs are created in the company.

b) Instance

An instance in a company is a body that makes decisions for subordinate bodies.

This means that the instance (job) precedes at least one job.

c) Hierarchy

The hierarchy of a company shows who is superior and who is subordinate in the company. Hierarchies can be flat or steep. Hierarchies usually adapt to the needs of companies and therefore have different characteristics. Flat hierarchies usually mean more decision-making authority and shorter decision-making paths. Steep hierarchies stand for a majority of superiors and more limited decisions of the individual positions / areas.

d) Centralization

In centralization in companies, one speaks when individual subtasks are combined centrally. Centralization can have various criteria and approaches for justification.

e) Decentralization

Decentralization is the alternative to centralization. In decentralization, combined subtasks are (again) broken down and managed as an independent area.

f) Job description

The job description is a written definition of the objectives, requirements, necessary qualifications, rights and obligations, etc. of a job. Inside the company, the job description is used as an instrument to describe a job as precisely as possible in order to fill it with the most suitable employee. The job description can also be used as a basis for externally visible job descriptions, e.g. on job portals. [23]

g) Organization chart

The organizational chart shows responsibilities (instances), areas, divisional management and the management according to their position in the company. Organizational chart figures are also called organizational forms. [24]

---

[23] Cf. Collier (2016): 46.

[24] Cf. Fischer, Unger (2001): 60.

The best-known forms of organization are:

- Line organization
- Staff positions
- Division organization/division organization/object-related organization
- Matrix organization
- Project organization

The line organization is shown here as an example. Other forms of organization can be quickly found by Google searches. These are not shown here, because it is supposed to be a help for startups. For startups, "large" structures are usually not yet necessary.

The line shows the organization hierarchical structure of an organization in line form. If there are several lines, all lines end at the top management level.

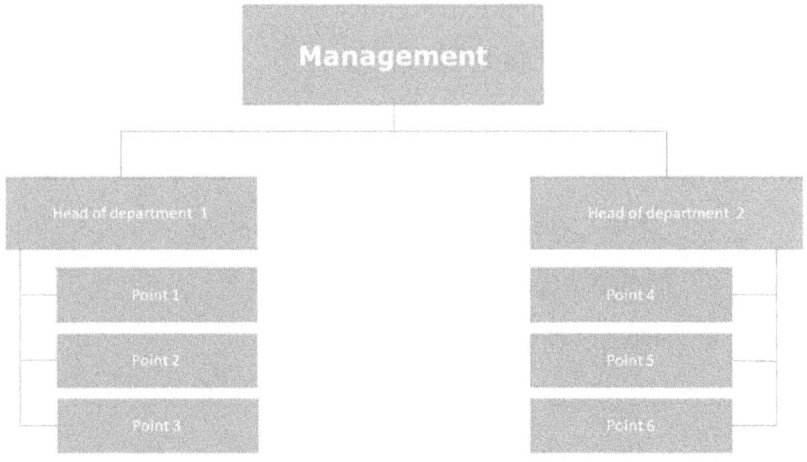

Figure 32 - line organization

h) Personnel planning

(a) Establishment plan

The position plan shows all required jobs in the company. In the position plan, it is not important whether they are occupied or not. The unfilled positions therefore also create a target status for the jobs. The target status is the best possible planned status.

(b) Staffing plan

Here, the position plan is displayed with all actual positions, i.e. occupied positions. If the staffing plan is not in line with the staffing plan, there is a need if the number of vacancies is too low, or a surplus if the number of vacancies is too high.

(b) Career planning

Career planning shows the possible career of an employee within the company. This can be influenced by further training or education as well as by gaining experience. The career plan is usually part of the personnel file.

Succession planning [3] Succession planning plans the succession of managers in advance. For this purpose, potential successors to the company are searched for and monitored further.

(c) Procurement planning

In procurement planning in personnel planning, the aim is to define

- What is to be achieved (objective, e.g. according to SMART more in 2.8)
- How it is to be achieved (measures, e.g. recruitment via temporary employment agencies) and
- With which resources it is to be achieved (how much capital and time may / should be used for it)

(d) Cost planning

The most important factor for planning point Personnel is the resource Capital. In personnel planning, it is important to take into account the fact that the revenues that new employees bring to the enterprise (usually, if they are not used to pursue another goal, such as image enhancement) should be greater than the costs incurred by new personnel.

IV.   Target group strategy

Strategy for dealing with the target group

The definition/size of the target group that is important for the business plan was already dealt with in 1.7.I. The information gained from 1.7.I. can also be used to define clusters. A cluster here stands for a group with uniform characteristics that form part of the target group.

Example:

- Yuppies - Young - Urban - Professional

(Young professionals / working people usually with a good income)

The advantage of defining such a group for yourself is that there are already many tips on how to deal with these particular clusters on the Internet.

2.8 Objectives of the strategy

STRATEGIC PLANNING

I. Definition of the goal of the strategy on which the entire enterprise is based

The definition of milestones can optimally support the overall goal setting.

Possible goals to be defined:

1. Operational goals = to be achieved in up to one year

2. Tactical goals = to reach in 1-3 years

3. Strategic goals = to be achieved in more than 3 years

In order to achieve time goals, according to the objectives or deadlines, there are various business tools, such as network plan technology or bar diagrams, which help to keep track of time through graphical figures.

Target definition must be measurable and accurate.

For example, the SMART definition can help:

S = specific: What exactly is the target?

M = measurable: data in measurable quantities (numbers)

A = attractive: is the goal desirable?

R = realizable: is the goal theoretical, logically achievable?

T = time can be set: time points for milestones, also for partial objectives [25]

Milestones help to see where deviations occur before the overall operational goal is set, for example, and thus map intermediate goals. Deviations or also the planned course can be read out by previously defined key figures.

---

[25] Cf. Niermeyer (2006): 46.

II. Relationship between strategic and operational planning

Strategic planning deals with long-term goals (usually up to 3 years), while operational planning deals with goals that are usually shorter than one year.

Strategic planning, thus defines the long-term main goal. Operational planning deals with short-term goals that are important within the strategic goals. Thus, operative planning is a downstream planning. Plans in operative planning are often only implemented in functional or partial areas. Thus, operative planning implements the whole in individual areas and individual subplans. Subplans usually include only parts of the business processes.

Examples of a segment plan include

- The production plan
- The research and development plan
- Sales plan
- Etc.

These sub-areas are important, but only a part of the whole. Combining the individual subplans into a whole is the overall planning.

a) Analysis of success potentials

If a company is able to bring a product or service to the market which offers a real benefit and thus forms the basis for success, it is a question of whether a competitive advantage can be achieved. This means that a good product/service will not automatically be successful, especially if similar or substitute products are more strongly represented and already better known on the market.

The analysis of success potentials is therefore about finding and defining a competitive advantage, especially vis-à-vis the market participants.

It is important to find out for which consumers and against which suppliers there is an advantage through one's Personal product/service. These advantages must always be communicated.

An example of how the analysis of success potentials can be used is, for example, the SWOT analysis.

III.   General corporate objectives

Examples of general corporate objectives:

- The best possible solution to customer problems
- Profit/maximization
- Securing liquidity
- Independence
- Social goals
- Ecological targets
- Securing the company's potential
- Self-realization of the founder

IV.   Securing liquidity

In business management, liquidity stands for the ability to meet payment obligations on time. In business administration, the aim is to have liquidity secured at all times in order to be able to pay personnel, suppliers, installments or other expenses. [26]It is important that liquidity is based on directly usable means of payment (usually money). Even if a company has large assets in the form of machines or buildings, it can go bankrupt if it cannot meet its payment obligations.

There are various formulas and degrees for calculating liquidity.

a) Calculation of static liquidity - Liquidity of 1st (L1), 2nd (L2) and 3rd (L3) degree

The liquidity ratios for the 1st, 2nd and 3rd liquidity ratios are calculated as follows:

$$L1 = \frac{\text{means of payment}}{\text{Current liabilities}} \times 100$$

$$L2 = \frac{\text{Cash equivalents + Current receivables}}{\text{Current liabilities}} \times 100$$

$$L3 = \frac{\text{Cash and cash equivalents + current receivables + inventories}}{\text{Current liabilities}} \times 100$$

---

[26] Cf. von Berkenstein (2011): 225.

Multiplying by 100 gives the percentage of the liquidity ratio. Receivables are receivables that the company expects to receive promptly from third parties. Inventories can be quickly converted into cash if necessary.

a) Liquidity plan

The aim of liquidity planning is to compare incoming payments and outgoing payments in order to see where differences arise. To do this, you need to know inpayments and outpayments.

Disbursements are, for example Rent, electricity, telephone, purchased goods, material, personnel, installments

Inpayments are e.g: Invoices that have been issued; other payments that are foreseeable.

If the inpayments are greater than the outpayments, there is a surplus.

If the outgoing payments are greater than the incoming payments, a requirement arises.

A demand is therefore a danger that endangers liquidity.

The liquidity plan therefore has the task of securing liquidity. It secures liquidity by disclosing or defining the incoming and outgoing payments, as well as a targeted control of activities in order to avoid possible bottlenecks.

b) The cash flow

The difference between cash inflows and outflows is also known as cash flow.

V. Accounting and controlling strategy

Is accounting/controlling to be treated as insourcing or out-sourcing?

In the case of insourcing: What needs to be considered?

- Define controlling areas and assign responsibilities
- Organize internal and external accounting

It is the task of "accounting" and controlling to constantly mon-itor, control, properly process and document figures in the company, regardless of how small or large a company is. The basis for this is always the incoming and outgoing payments and a good planning of these.

Accounting - or even parts of it - can possibly be outsourced, especially for small companies. Various online offers show that this is a common practice. The advantages of outsourcing are time savings and concentration on one's Personal core competencies. Nevertheless, it is important to know the basic nature of accounting in order to have an overview.

VI. Corporate identity, corporate culture and corporate philosophy

a) Corporate Identity

Corporate Identity is a long-term, described ideal image and describes an ideal behavior in the future (also in the immediate future). It is valid for all areas in the company, is basically feasible and in itself contradiction-free.

The corporate identity wants to convey its Personal special image. The CI is translated as corporate identity. [27]

The corporate identity is divided into three sub-areas.

---

[27] Cf. Kiessling, Babel (2016): 23.

b) Corporate Design

It is about the unique and unmistakable external appearance like logo, business cards, packaging design, (depending on size) company headquarters, company vehicles, etc. In the Corporate Identity this point is called Corporate Design. Already mentioned in 2.6.

c) Corporate Communication

In corporate communication, the communication strategy is defined by which internal and external communication is to take place. Corporate communication is used internally for communications to employees as well as externally for advertising measures, for example.

d) Corporate Behavior

Corporate Behavior is closely linked to Corporate Communication. This is about the tone of contact and the expression of behavior, both internally and externally. Behavior is not only expressed through words (which are regulated in corporate communication), but also through direct action. It concerns values of the personnel policy, purchase policy, etc. of the enterprise.

e) Goals of the Corporate Identity

Through the uniqueness of its Personal identity, which is created by the CI, a company pursues the goal of shaping its external perception.

It is important for all market participants to present themselves as an unmistakable company. A Personal image and a Personal appearance develop, which should differentiate itself from all other market participants.

If a company is a legal entity, it is treated legally as if it was its Personal person. The corporate identity gives this "person" its character.

For employees, the CI offers the advantage of knowing the clear overall objectives in terms of design, behavior and communication and thus having more orientation.

2.9 improvement strategies

STRATEGIC PLANNING

I.   Strategy for dealing with risks

By defining a comprehensive risk catalogue, you are better prepared for the risks and can take advantage of opportunities that are identified as a result.

The risk catalogue can be created using the Entrepreneur Matrix. Submatrices can be created for each topic of the matrix, such as the risk matrix below. The risk matrix can always be extended in order to counteract as many risks as possible or to be able to adjust to them.

3.3 Risk matrix

A sub-matrix is a matrix that is applied to a specific topic. All fields therefore refer to the name of the matrix. Since there is no main field, all nine fields are treated in a sub-matrix. Sub-matrices can be helpful to deepen a topic. More examples of submatrices can be found in chapter 10. A submatrix is also suitable for brainstorming purposes.

Risk matrix 1

I. Risks related to the product/service

The risks associated with the product/service can be identified and minimized or prevented by asking specific questions.

Examples:

- Could someone injure themselves or suffer damage to the product?
- Can someone be injured unintentionally during the provision of the service (e.g. By tools lying around)?

After identifying the risk, it should be clarified:

How can risks be prevented?

Possible countermeasures are e.g:

- TÜV/DIN inspections
- Occupational safety instructions for employees

II. Manufacturing risks

The aim here is to identify possible problems / risks during production.

Possible countermeasures are e.g:

Analyze manufacturing processes, e.g. on the basis of the cause-effect diagram.

The cause-effect diagram, the herringbone diagram or the Ishikawa diagram is a problem diagnosis technique.

a) The Ishikawa diagram

The cause-effect diagram systematically analyzes the causes of errors. The cause-effect diagram deals with at least 6 general sources of error

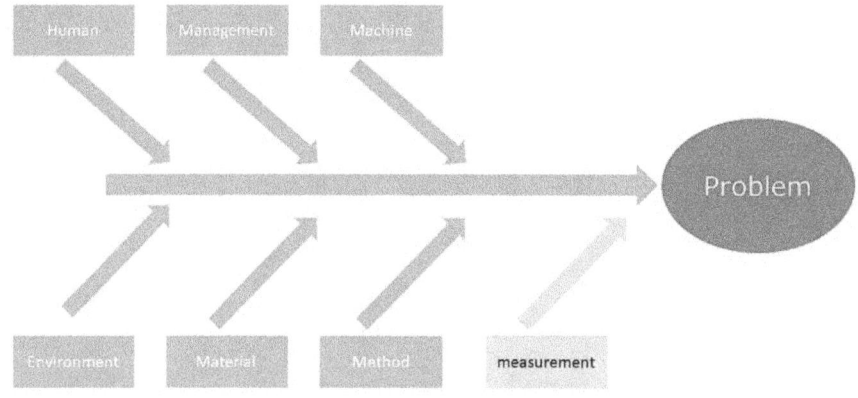

Figure 34 – Ishikawa-Diagram

milieu stands for the environment. Depending on the literature, the 7th "M" for measurement and the 8th "M" for money
are added. If the main causes (one of the M) are found, secondary causes are searched for and found by the W-ques-
tions (like, who, where, with what, why, etc.) and the solutions
are derived. These secondary causes are attached to the
"bones" in a graphical representation such as ABB. 35. Possible causes can of course be individualized, because the 6
"M" and 8'"M" listed here are only typical examples.[28]

---

[28] Cf. Jochem / Giebel (2011): 178.

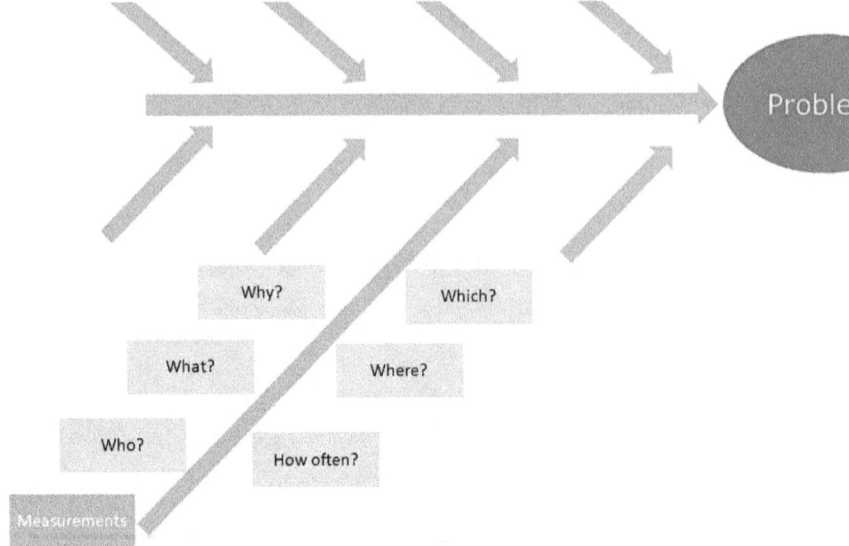

Figure 35 – W- Questions/Ishikawa

Risk matrix 2

I.   Risks related to strategy

The aim here is to identify possible risks in relation to the strategy.

Examples:

- What deviations could there be?
- How should deviations be dealt with?
- What effects can changes have on other areas?

Possible countermeasures are e.g:

To scan the environment regularly through regular analyzes (e.g. PESTEL analyzes).

Risk Matrix 3

I. Financial risks

Identify financial risks that may apply to the business. In principle, all cost factors are associated with the risk of cost increases.

Examples and possible countermeasures:

- Cost increase with advertising partners - e.g. should this be counteracted by planning additional finances or by contractual commitments (agreements in writing as a contract, but this is often not possible with large platforms)?
- Cost increase for consultants - (planning of additional finances / contractual commitment (if possible))
- The company has start-up difficulties and does not generate any income in the first few months - this can be counteracted by planning in reserves.

II. Invoices are not paid on time

Invoices that are not paid on time can endanger liquidity and thus the entire company.

Possible countermeasures are:

- Cooperation with debt collection companies to collect receivables
- Sale of receivables to factoring companies
- Obtain data on the buyer (Schufa information) in the Vor-Field. This is often the case with B2B.
- Pay in advance

Risk Matrix 4

I. Legal risks

The legal framework is always risky. Noncompliance, non-observance, lack of knowledge in this area or negligent handling of laws or behavior prescribed by law can quickly lead to high (avoidable) costs.

An exemplary list of frequent risks that can arise from the above-mentioned behavior:

- Product liability
- Patent infringements
- Trademark infringements
- Domain grabbing (abusive active use or reservation of a domain)
- New laws
- New regulations (e.g. Data protection regulation)
- Imprint obligation
- All warnings
- Not enough legal protection for Personal products

Possible countermeasures to counteract this are:

- Search (can also be carried out by third parties)
- Legal (re) examination (also recommended for web-sites), permanent legal observation
- To seek further views on difficult areas
- Din exams
- Etc.

II. Risks arising from the behavior of the competitor(s)

The aim here is to identify possible risks from competitors.

- Assessing the "mood" of the competitor. Is this already clouded or is the competitor losing market share?
- What could the competitor plan? What steps could the competitor take?
- What is the worst case that could happen to "our" company?
- Possible countermeasures to counteract this are:
- Analysis of how to counteract possible actions of the competitor
- Identify weaknesses of the competitor for yourself

Risk Matrix 5

I. Risks with sales platforms and the location

a) Identify risks related to the sales platform

Examples:

- Conversion of platform structures

- Change in commissions

b) Identify site-related risks

Examples:

- The legal situation changes for productions abroad

- Neighbors complain about noise

I. Risks related to advertising

Identify all possible risks associated with advertising.

Examples and possible countermeasures:

- The chosen channels reach the target group worse than expected - find out how restructuring is possible and what other possibilities there are.
- Key advertising figures sound the alarm, e.g. the opening rates of e-mail marketing. Countermeasures must be sought (e.g. Whitelisting - can help prevent mass e-mails from ending up in spam folders. Whitelisting is possible, e.g. by external providers to send mass mails. Example: https://www.newsletter2go.de).

Risk Matrix 7

I.   Risks related to personnel/target group

Determine the risks that can arise from the personnel, the target group and already from the target group analysis.

Example:

- The purchasing behavior of the target group was wrongly evaluated. The target group prefers to buy second-hand instead of new goods.

Possibilities for a solution:

Restructuring to another / extended

Target audience

Risk Matrix 8

I.   Risks of non-achievement of objectives

By setting a goal, there is always the risk that this goal cannot be achieved. Virtually every area that has a goal or has an influence on the goals is exposed to this risk of not achieving the goal.

a) The competition is too strong against the current marketing strategy

Countermeasures:

Change your Personal behavior.

Using Meffert's behavioral theories.

These are:

- Avoidance strategy: Attempting to "avoid" the competitor. Here, for example, innovative advertising strategies can be used to avoid direct contact.

- Conflict strategy: the conflict strategy is specifically about gaining market shares from the competitor for your Personal company.
- Adjustment strategy: the aim here is to adapt one's Personal products to those of the competitors.
- Cooperation strategy: the cooperation strategy tries to co-operate with the competitor. E.g. on a contractual basis.[29]

b) The milestones set show a large deviation from the target value

- How to deal with it?
- What strategies need to be changed?
- What could be the reason?

Countermeasures:

Check whether key figures have not been generated or only insufficiently generated, and whether this has subsequently resulted in too little control. If this is the case, possible countermeasures would be here: The installation of a key figure

---

[29] Cf. Rennhak (2017): 108 ff.

system and its constant control (by obliging a suitable person).

c) Problems with time management or deadlines are not met

Times or the corresponding duration of certain processes, etc. result from the planning of work to be carried out. Since planning is a forecast, it can quickly lead to deviations. Negative deviations can cause problems in other areas. Orders, for example, cannot be fulfilled punctually or even not at all. Contractual penalties or the loss of customers can quickly become a risk due to inadequate time management. The following points are about how to act when "the child has already fallen into the well".

Examples and countermeasures

- Do important things that cannot be postponed first. The Eisenhower Principle (see (a)) can help here.
- Analyze and give priority to customers who are important for the company's portfolio. For example, the ABC analysis (see (b)) is suitable as an analysis.

- Projector parts influence other parts negatively in terms of time. Here visualizations of the project can help to recognize critical areas. These visualizations can be found, for example, in the Gant-diagram.

(a) The Eisenhower Principle

The Eisenhower principle helps to classify tasks in a matrix in order to get an overview for yourself. The matrix can then be used to first process tasks that are urgent and visible.[30]

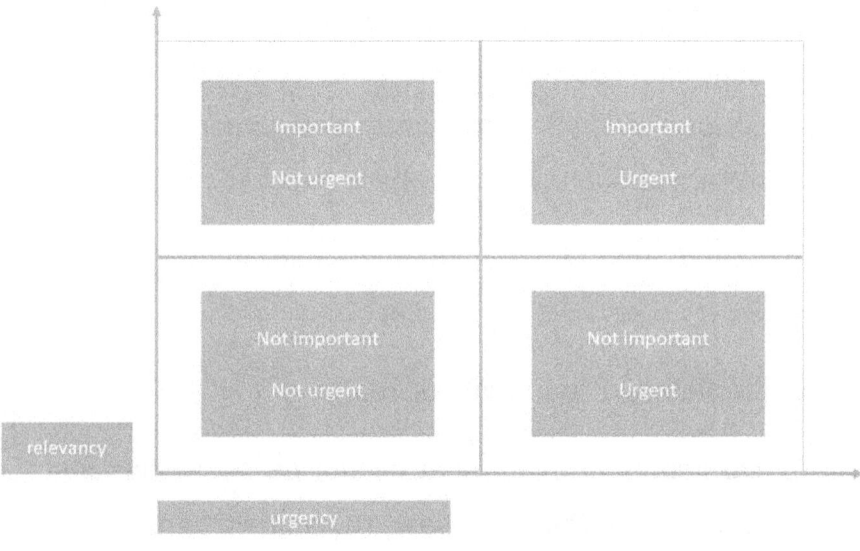

Figure 36 – Eisenhower Principle

---

[30] Cf. Züger (2007): 58.

(b) The ABC analysis

ABC analysis is a business method for dividing objects into three categories (A, B or C)

Customers, products, suppliers, parts or other analysis objects can each be assigned to one category.

Importance of the categories for the company:

A = very important for the company

B = important for the company

C = less important for the company

The ABC analysis helps to use resources, purposefully in order to achieve the best possible situation for the company. This means that, especially when bottlenecks occur, Category C content, which is less important for the company, is dispensed with first. The ABC analysis is often found in time management, because the resource time is limited. [31]

---

[31] Cf. Züger (2007): 55.

Determination of the ABC analysis

The ABC analysis determines its categories according to existing figures - i.e. according to easily measurable criteria. An example would be the turnover for customers and the contribution margin for products.

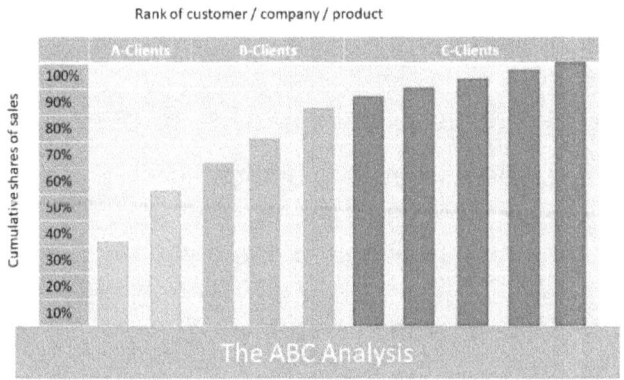

Figure 37 – ABC analysis

With the ABC analysis the customers or products are sorted according to the size of the turnover shares, as can be seen on the chart. This means, for example, that the customer with the highest turnover is an A customer.

With existing statistics, etc., the ABC analysis can be easily prepared and also graphically displayed. This can be helpful for presentations and or decision making.

(c) Pareto principle

This famous principle, which is not only used in the economy, goes back to Vilfrido Pareto (1848-1923).

The Pareto principle is a 20-80 rule that says that e.g. 80% of the work can be done in 20% of the time. Or 20% of the customer's account for 80% of the turnover.

In fact, in time management it is often 20% of the work that takes 80% of the time. The Pareto principle in time management could analyze the tedious 20% of the work and check their meaningfulness. Perhaps the resources could be used better to serve e.g. A-customers better.

(d) Gantt chart or also bar chart

The Gantt diagram is one way of displaying the timing of processes in a project. The Gantt chart names the tasks and the timeframe. Lines and arrows can also be used to display dependencies. A Gantt diagram is thus a table with "bars" that graphically represent the duration of project parts.

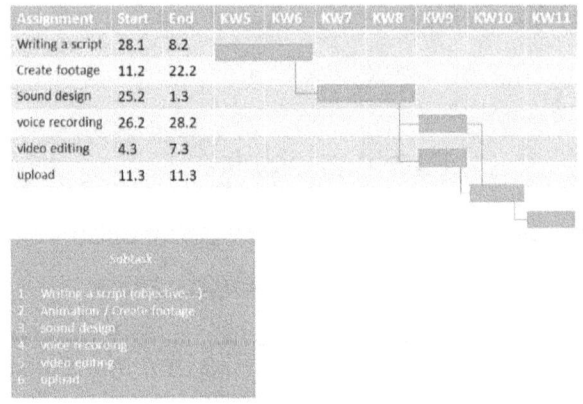

Figure 38 - bar chart

Risk Matrix 9

I. Risks of improvements/innovations

Innovations, improvements, but also changes to a product or service also entail risks. These must be determined in advance and, if necessary, countermeasures planned.

Examples and countermeasures:

- What are the legal risks associated with new innovations? It is important to clarify the legal situation before a possible (new) start. An example of this is product liability for modified products.
- The research for innovation takes too much time and financial resources - a possible solution would be to redefine and adhere to the budget. Of course, costs and benefits have to be compared.

3.4 Field 3 – Financial planning

FINANCIAL PLANNING

3.1 Cost analysis for the product/service

FINANCIAL PLANNING

I.   Cost analysis

Field 1.3 was concerned with whether the product/service was financially feasible in principle. Now it is about whether there is profit potential. At this point, data from 1.3 and 2.3 (pricing strategy) must be used in order to have them in mind for further consolidation.

A first deepening with regard to the profit potential is possible, e.g. through a contribution margin analysis (here only contribution margin 1 is discussed) or break-even point analysis.

a) The contribution margin

The contribution margin is a controlling instrument for the short-term income statement.

The contribution margin (DB) distinguishes between the contribution margin, the single-level contribution margin and the multi-level contribution margin.

The contribution margin results from this:

Sales revenue (per unit) - variable costs (per unit) = contribution margin per unit

b) Break-even point

The break-even point is the point at which the company begins to make a profit. It thus describes the sales quantity at which the sales revenue covers the costs.

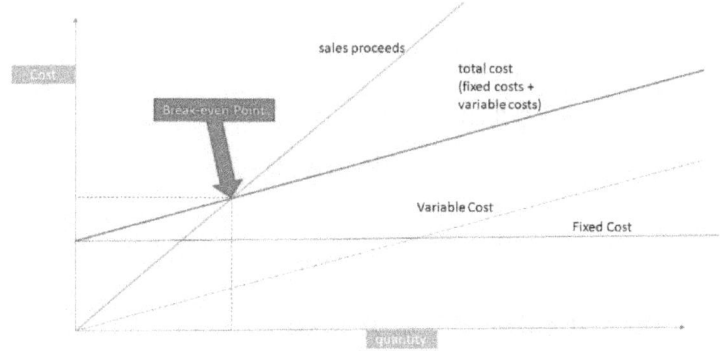

Figure 39 – break-even point [32]

The costs that form the intersection with the sales revenue are the total costs, that is, fixed costs and variable costs. The break-even point is also known as the break-even point.

The formula for the break-even point quantity is as follows:

Fixed costs : Piece contribution margin

= Profit threshold quantity

[32] Cf. Vry (2017): 315.

From this formula it can be deduced how large the sales volume must be in order to reach the break-even point. In order to represent the minimum sales in monetary terms, the profit threshold quantity can be multiplied by the sales price.

II.   The minimum sales volume

From the break-even point it can be determined how large the sales volume of a company must be at least for the company to be worthwhile at all.

This minimum sales volume must then be compared with the "market". Is there enough demand on the market for the calculated minimum sales volume? For this purpose, questions have to be asked, among other things:

- Is it possible to sell x-pieces at all?
- Is there enough demand?
- Is my target group large enough?
- Can I assert myself against my competitors?
- Can advertising be used to draw attention to the product/service in such a way that a minimum sales volume is achieved?

III.   Relative contribution margin

Relative contribution margin is the contribution margin in relation to a bottleneck.

The relative contribution margin can be important in a production. The point here is to check which products should be given priority in the event of a bottleneck and how high an output quantity can be.

The formula is as follows:

Contribution margin per unit : Bottleneck utilization per unit

The bottleneck utilization limits the number of units by the time factor.

Example:

A child's bed needs 60 minutes on a milling machine. The workshop is open for 8 hours. The contribution margin is 100 Euro.

Due to the bottleneck:

100 Euro: 1 (as 1 piece per hour)

= 100 Euro per hour relative contribution margin

If you work 8 hours, the relative DB is 800 EUR

3.2 Financing strategy

FINANCIAL PLANNING

I. Financing planning

Determine where and how the company is to be financed.

a) Debt financing

Examples of external financing (external financing):

- Support programs (DE/EU/)
- Bank loan (house bank or KFW)
- Private loans/micro credits
- Overdraft facility (credit from credit institution to current account to bridge bottlenecks)

- Crowdfunding
- Loans from investors
- Payments against investor shareholdings
- Leasing

b) Self-financing

Examples of self-financing (internal financing)

- Financing from Personal funds
- Investments (e.g. In investment companies or capital increases in a company)

For founders

Particularly in the case of startups, the personal contribution can be an important prerequisite for setting up a business. The listing of equity capital also has a major influence on loans that may become necessary in the course of the business venture. The reason for this is that the banks analyze the economic activity through this list and only lead to an approval if the assessment is positive.

The description of the assets that are to flow into the enterprise can take place in financial means or also in the equipment (country-specific equipment is possible as equivalent value to the contribution into the enterprise assets).

II.   Reasons for financing

Even existing companies need (mostly) "fresh" money to develop/grow. An example would be the development and introduction of a new product.

At this point, a distinction is made between financing for start-up, expansion investments and replacement investments. Replacement investments are needed, for example, if machines, etc. becomes worn out or even unable to work.

Financing can be raised for the whole company or for a project.

3.4 Costs for legal factors

FINANCIAL PLANNING

I. Costs for all legal factors of the enterprise

This field should represent an exemplary list of costs, which concern the legal framework of the entire enterprise.

Examples:

- Costs for industrial property rights:
- Patents
- Trademark application

- Design protection
- the search before filing the application
- legal advice
- lawyer's fee (should the registration of patents, etc. be done by a lawyer)

Costs of incorporation:

- Registration/registration of the company
- other charges connected with registration
- Possible compulsory levies (country-specific)
- contracts/articles of association necessary for the foundation

Other legal costs:

- Legal protection (if possible in the country)
- DIN tests
- Costs for legal security on the Internet - e.g. data protection regulations

3.5 Costs for sales platform/location

FINANCIAL PLANNING

I. Costs for the respective sales platforms and location

After the positioning, the costs for the Personal location and the sales platform (the place where the company is made visible) can be derived and listed here.

 ## Costs for locations

Which locations entail which costs?

Examples:

- The office/branch (rent/purchase and ancillary costs)

- Production halls (hire/purchase and ancillary costs)

- Parts and logistics warehouse (hire/purchase and ancillary costs)

 **Costs for sales platform**

Which platform entails which costs?

Examples:

- Costs for Hosting/Website

- Costs for setup/adjustment fees on platforms

- Support costs

- Costs for platform-specific specifications (e.g. The obligation to provide quality advertising clips and product images)

3.6 Advertising costs

FINANCIAL PLANNING

I.   Advertising costs

The prices for advertising can usually be researched online or must be obtained through offers. Prices usually consist of the display prices and the creation costs + other costs (e.g. Setup fees).

Examples:

- Print costs
- Costs for online advertising
- Prices for SEO Optimization

- Thousand-Contact-Price (TKP)

How high do reserves have to be planned in order to maintain the advertising strategy, e.g. in case of start-up difficulties?

II. Costs for market introduction and permanent advertising campaigns

There are advertising costs of market launch and permanent promotions.

The individual promotions should be planned separately, since a market launch usually requires an increased advertising presence.

III. Graphic costs

Costs for graphic works that come about in 1.6 and 2.6.

Examples:

- Product logo
- Company logo
- Business cards
- Letterhead
- Slogan design
- Packagings
- Design guidelines (CD)

3.7 Costs for employees

FINANCIAL PLANNING

I.   Employee costs

If the company is run full-time, in addition to the costs for employees, the costs for one's Personal livelihood/further education must be planned and possibly secured by a loan.

Examples

- What is the current net amount? (If an employment relationship currently exists)
- What must one's Personal minimum wage be in order to maintain one's standard of living? What can be done without?
- How large are the reserves for a living?
- What do the employees receive (gross salary)?
- How high are the ancillary wage costs?
- What does possible further training courses cost?
- What does vacation time cost?
- What do average sick days cost the entrepreneur?
- What do freelancers cost?
- What do employees cost via temporary employment agencies?

If necessary, costs for freelancers and permanent employees can be compared in order to identify potential savings in a company.

3.8 Costs for controlling, financial accounting and accounting

FINANCIAL PLANNING

I.   Costs for Controlling & Co.

Determine costs for tax consultants, financial consultants, bookkeeping and controlling, plus offers from tax consultants, etc. (as required) obtain

In addition to daily requirements, there are areas that cause one-off costs each year, such as completing the annual financial statements and the income statement, and possibly also the balance sheet and income statement for larger compa-nies. For projects: How much does the additional expense of accounting/controlling costs?

3.9 Costs for improvements

FINANCIAL PLANNING

I. Costs for research & development (R&D), optimization, identification of innovation

Investment in research, development, optimization and innovation must be regular. Resources such as capital and time have to be planned. If nothing is planned for these areas, it will be difficult to invest in them.

The implementation phase:

In the implementation phase (here parenthesis 2), the first 3 planning fields (here parenthesis 1) do not exist. Planning is completed here. For the following implementation the planning remains naturally relevant and forms the foundation of the enterprise. Possible new findings that arise in the implementation phase and influence the planning phase can be retroactively improved in the respective planning fields.

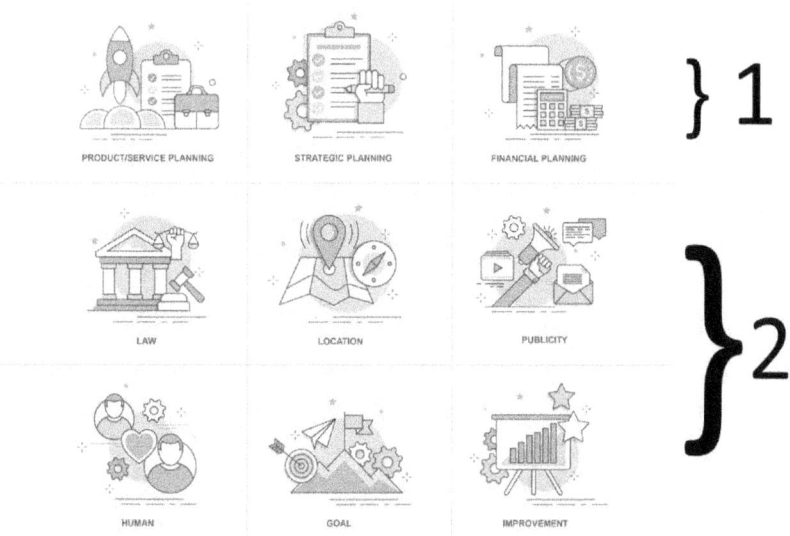

Figure 41 – Planning phase and implementation phase of the matrix

Since the planning phase after Field 3 has been completed, only the 6 practical fields are relevant in the implementation phase. One field of the implementation phase is now explained by the remaining 5 fields.

3.5 Field 4 – Law

LAW

4.5 Platforms (places) for laws and legal aspects

LAW

I. Platforms for researching laws, legal framework conditions and entrepreneurial obligations

This is about the legal framework for the entire company.

Examples for the search of trademarks, patents and utility models

- www.tmdb.de (Germany/search for trademarks - also Europe-wide and (partly) US trademarks)

- https://www.dpma.de/recherche/ (German Patent and Trade Mark Office)
- Example USA for brands: www.uspto.gov/trademarks-application-process/search-trademark-database
- https://euipo.europa.eu/ohimportal/de/databases (Intellectual Property Office of the European Union)
- https://www.wipo.int/branddb/en/ (World Intellectual Property Organization)

Trademarks, patents & Co. can also be registered internationally (e.g. IR trademarks). Therefore, it makes sense to check in the VorField whether the trademark/patent etc. exists abroad. If an expansion abroad is planned, a search should also be carried out in the country concerned and a possible entry made abroad, e.g. via WIPO.

Domestic registrations also give rise to (country-specific) registration priorities, so that registration deadlines can be shortened.

This point is also interesting for companies from the service sector, if, for example, franchises are being considered. Particularly with service providers close to the border, the observance of cross-border names can have advantages.

c) Examples of platforms which represent entrepreneurial obligations are country-specific laws and associated obligations.

Examples from the research of German laws, which are relevant for many (German) enterprises:

- Consumer protection - www.gesetze-im-internet.de/vschdg/
- Consumer goods purchases - consumer goods purchases are regulated by the consumer protection and by the paragraph § 474 BGB (one can investigate laws on the Internet, e.g.: https://www.gesetze-im-internet.de/bgb/__474.html)
- Right of withdrawal for consumer contracts - § 355 BGB (German Civil Code)
- Inclusion and content control of AGB - § 305 BGB (German Civil Code)
- Possession and ownership - § 854 BGB, § 903 BGB
- Further important regulations to possession and property - § 868 BGB

Note: A clause stating that the buyer is the owner only after full payment can be very important for founders. In contracts, legal assistance can bring many advantages. Specialist lawyers should always be consulted on the required topics.

4.6 Advertising through the legal framework

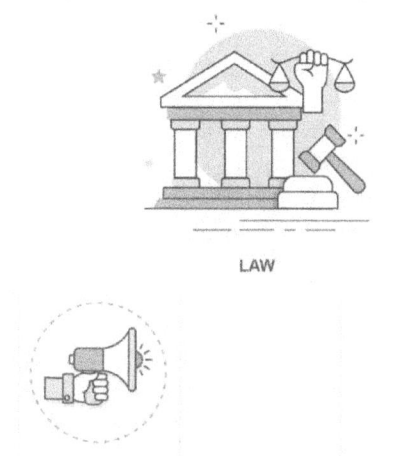

LAW

I. Identifying advertising opportunities

The legal framework of an enterprise can bring advertising possibilities with it. Slogans like, "with our patented system", ®, "original trademark" or seal, which are subject to legal regulations like the bio seal can bring a large advertising effect with it.

4.7 Target group and staff for the legal framework

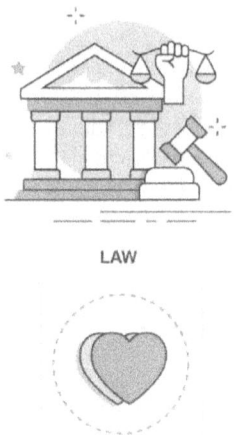

LAW

 Target audience

I. For which persons are the company's Personal legal framework relevant?

Defining the target group as precisely as possible can help to take specific aspects into account and to communicate them in a targeted manner.

Examples:

- Other companies (legal entities) - if no intellectual property rights exist, (good) ideas can simply be copied
- Rechtsanwälte - Competitors can issue warnings via lawyers. Warnings concern legal weak points in an enterprise (e.g. Imprint obligation on the Personal web page)
- Customers - a registered trademark or patented system reflects a competent, innovative company

 Staff

II. Staffing needs arising from the legal framework

Here the question arises: Should work be carried out within the company or externally in relation to the legal framework?

Examples:

- What does legal expenses insurance cover? Is it possible/meaningful to take out legal expenses insurance?
- Is a separate legal department required?
- Is it possible to work externally with a consultant lawyer?

4.8 Objectives with the legal framework

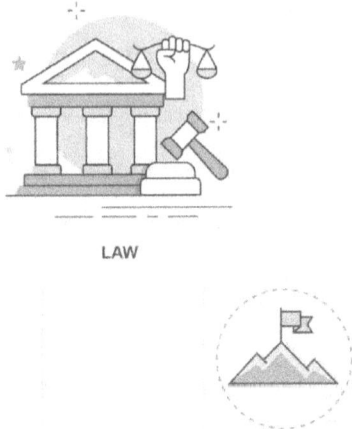

LAW

I. What is the company's Personal goal with the legal framework?

Here it is clarified why the legal framework is relevant for the company. Any legal protection must be justified because it also offers a target.

Examples

- Why do I need patent protection?
- Why do I need multiple domains?
- Why do I need design protection?

- Is it about really protecting something or is it just for the patent? (Some founders file many utility models, but do not use them. This makes them vulnerable to possible warnings from outside.)

4.9 Improving the legal aspects

LAW

I.   Check whether there is room for improvement with regard to the legal aspects.

The accompanying process of the constant search for improvement should run in all areas of a company. Improvements help to seize opportunities and minimize risks. For example, the search and identification of legal improvements can help to create an advantageous position in relation to the competition.

Examples:

- Deletion of unused property rights
- Extension of intellectual property rights

3.6 Field 5 – Location

LOCATION

Basically, as mentioned in the introduction, this field is divided into two parts.

In the subfields of Field 5 there is a division into sales platforms and branch offices.

Every company, no matter how small or large, has both factors. Each enterprise has a registered office (base/subsidiary) and each enterprise must meet somewhere on the market (sales platform(s)).

Every self-employed person has a workplace (thus a branch), even if it is only a laptop.

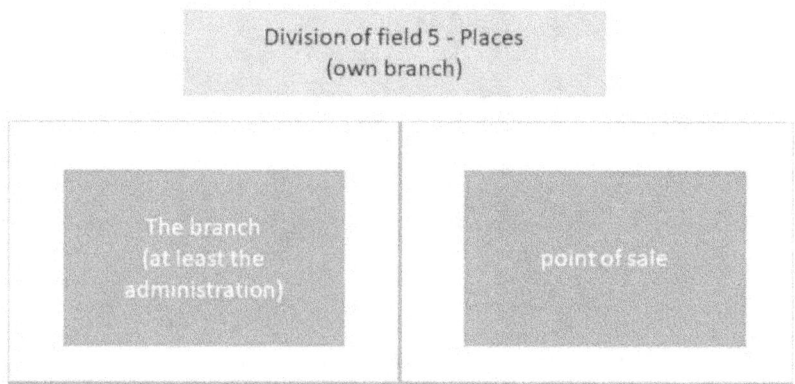

Figure 42 – Division of the Field 5

- The branch

- The point of sale

The branch can also be divided into three areas:

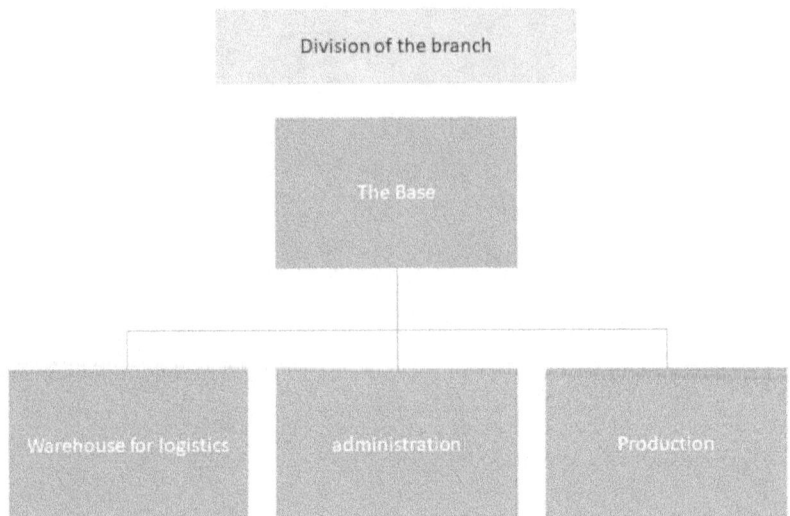

Figure 43 – Division of the branch

1. Warehouse for logistics - the warehouse (also often needed by service companies) is often located at its Personal location.

2. Administration - Includes, unless outsourced, e.g. sales, accounting/controlling, advertising, legal, human resources, research & development and management. In the case of

startups or self-employed persons, these areas are often handled by one and the same person.

3. Production - with Personal production the production often has its Personal place.

5.4 Platform-specific/location-specific rights

LOCATION

 **Points of sale**

I. Platform-specific rights

Each platform has its Personal Terms of Service and its Personal legal framework. The location of each platform can have an impact on legal aspects, as legislation varies from country to country.

Examples:

- Read contracts with platforms thoroughly

- Clarify product liability/transfer of liability
- Observe imprint obligation
- Who is the registered seller when selling through a platform?
- Research other legal events

Branch

II. Rights bound to a specific location

A location has its Personal legal framework. These must be observed.

Examples:

- Rental and sales contracts and the associated rights and obligations
    - If necessary, contracts with logistics partners
    - If necessary, contracts with suppliers (for in-house production)
    - If necessary contracts with caretaker service/cleaners
    - Noise protection/rest periods regulations, if applicable

5.6 Advertising on platforms and through branch offices

LOCATION

 **Points of sale**

I. Advertising opportunities on sales platforms

Depending on the platform, new, unused advertising opportunities can be identified through research. At Amazon, for example, the quality of the text content (content) can improve the search results even without advertising by the Amazon marketing service. Similarly, when companies are entered into Google, images or company films up-loaded by each user or the owner himself can also improve the search results without Google AdWords (paid advertising).

Examples:

- Advertisements/Banners
- SEO
- Keywords
- Content
- Pictures
- Movies/Clips
- Coupon actions
- Ratings
- Reviews

Branch

II. Advertising possibilities through the branch office

The fact that the company has its Personal location creates advertising opportunities, the benefits of which should be weighed up.

Examples:

- Vehicle lettering
- Posters (e.g. Also on fences)
- Outdoor advertising
- Company signs
- Labeling of shop windows

5.7 Target group and staff of the platforms

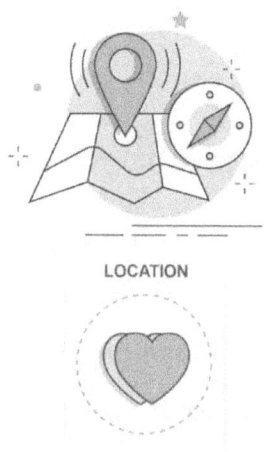

LOCATION

 Target audience:

 **Points of sale**

I. Target groups for the respective sales platform

It is important to check whether the target group of a chosen platform matches the Personal target group defined for the product/service. Example: On the sales platform ETSY mainly

214

customers are to be found, who look for individual and self-made things. Industrially produced things would find a very limited target group there.

Branch

I. Target group around the branch/company

Questions can be used in the pre-field to define the persons around the branch in order to draw conclusions from them if necessary.

Question **example**:

- What is the situation in the environment like?
- Is there potential for conflict with local residents, e.g. due to increased traffic volume (cars/trucks), machine noise, etc.?

Staff

 **Points of sale**

I. Personnel requirements for the use of sales platforms

Is more personnel needed to use the platform?

Offering a product/service on a platform can be a significant effort due to many regulations. Graphic templates of the design scope can limit online platforms. This applies to the manufacturing industry (e.g. Amazon) and to service companies, for which various example works have to be presented on platforms.

If there is a high additional demand, it must be checked whether this corresponds to the available time resources. A separate time management system is of great importance for every company.

Branch

II. Personnel expenses for the branch office

For (larger) locations:

How large is the additional personnel expenditure?

Examples:

- Cleaning staff
- Secretariat/Reception
- Exterior care of company facilities

Repeat:

Production personnel should be defined for the different scenarios in the product description (1/3).

5.8 Goals for the platforms and the Personal location

LOCATION

 **Points of sale**

I. Target definition with the respective sales platform

Defining the target as precisely as possible in figures (defining key figures) and in the best case with milestones defined over time can help to reschedule deviations if necessary.

Example:

 **Manufacturing industry**

- 350 units sold within 60 days

Service industry

- 25 new customers per month via the platform

 Branch

I. Goals with the Personal basis

The choice of the extent of one's Personal base should always be justified. Goals are helpful in becoming aware of these aspects.

Examples:

• Creating effective workplaces

- Ensure proper disposal, e.g. by collection, separation of waste, etc.
- An advantage over the alternative use of the branch office

II. If applicable, goal of Personal logistics (distribution policy goals)

Examples of general objectives of logistics:

- Reduction of distribution costs
- High degree of readiness to deliver
- Increase in market share
- Increase in sales
- Guarantee of loading security
- Guarantee of on-schedule goods issue

a) The "6R"

It is important to note here that it is all about logistics - including internal logistics - and not just logistics to the customer.

The aim of logistics is to fulfil its basic tasks, which are also described as the "6Rs":

- Correct objects (products)
- Right amount
- Right moment
- Real place
- Write quality
- Right costs [33]

---

[33] Cf. Roux (2015): 3.

5.9 Improvements around the locations/platforms

LOCATION

 **Points of sale**

I. Possibilities of improvement on the sales platform

A good advertising strategy makes this point superfluous. In addition to the advertising strategy, personal discussions with buyers and traders can also help to improve your Personal positions. The reason for it lies in the feedback and the realizations won from it, which can be won by simple questions, which a simple advertising strategy would not have given here.

Branch

I. Goals of improvement with one's Personal basis

An independent basis, regardless of its size, always has potential for improvement due to its independence. Depending on the size of the company, this improvement may be more or less pronounced. In addition, the market for external production, external warehouses, etc. should be observed in order to take advantage of emerging opportunities or to counteract risks - such as significant price increases for external production - in good time.

Example:

- Regular checks to see whether more or more waste can be avoided.
- The possibilities for this could be, for example:
- Reusable packaging
- Improvement/adjustment of the product design
- The packaging design
- Check reusability or reusability of wastes (of course with retention of legal framework conditions)
- Is another location more suitable for the base?
- Are there any ideas for improvements to operational processes?

3.7 Field 6 - Publicity

PUBLICITY

6.4 The legal framework around advertising

PUBLICITY

I.   Relevant laws/legal framework relating to advertising

Creativity in advertising helps to stand out from the competition. But creativity can (unconsciously) violate the rights of others. Thus, this field deals with possible risks that may arise from the legal framework around advertising.

Examples:

- Find out whether competitors' keywords may be used to launch an AdWords campaign - this should also be checked for international advertising. In case of doubt, legal advice is highly recommended.
- Paying attention to possible contributions to the artists' social security fund - when working with "creative people" this should be checked.
- Certain advertising procedures are prohibited in certain countries because they are unfair. There are the principles of competition law, e.g. in the law against unfair competition (in Germany) (https://www.gesetze-im-internet.de/uwg_2004/).

Examples from the German UWG:

- comparative advertising
- false information in advertising
- aggressive sales methods
- unclear information in promotional contests and sweepstakes
- conceal one's Personal identity in advertising brochures, etc.

- no agreements with companies that are actually in competition (at least not without appropriate involvement of consumers / §2 GWB[34]

---

[34] Cf. Gesetz gegen den unlauteren Wettbewerb § 2.

6.5 Platforms/Places for Advertising

PUBLICITY

I. Higher-level platforms for the provision of services on the subject of advertising

The aim here is to find platforms on which information on the subject of advertising can be found as cheaply and as accurately as possible.

Examples:

- Platforms for the production of Flyern, all diagram services, E-Mail marketing and account care of e.g. Social Media appearances (e.g. www.fiverr.com language-unspecific)

- Pages for tenders, e.g. for flyers, advertising clips, apps, finding names, etc. (e.g. www.designenlassen.de)
- Platforms for free images that can also be used for commercial purposes (e.g. www.pixabay.de)
- Platforms for fonts with costs, but also free fonts, which can be suitable for advertising purposes (e.g. www.dafont.com)

II.   Possibility of affiliate marketing

Affiliate marketing = partner advertising

A company uploads advertising material on the platform of an affiliate agency. These advertisements can be downloaded by website operators and published on the operator's site. If a visitor clicks on the advertising media, the website operator usually receives a percentage commission of the purchased product/service. The affiliate agency uses a module implemented in the back office of the corporate website to track where the buyer came from.

Examples of advertising material on affiliate platforms are:

- Banner advertising
- Text links
- Coupon codes (Very interesting for coupon sites)
- Blogs (Entries PR)
- Email marketing

A big advantage of affiliate marketing is that many providers offer a model that only has to be paid for once the sale has taken place. This payment is called pay-per-sale. Alternatively, there is also the frequent payment method Pay-per-Click, in which the seller has to pay when his ad is only clicked, as in Google AdWords.

6.7 Personnel and target group aspects for advertising

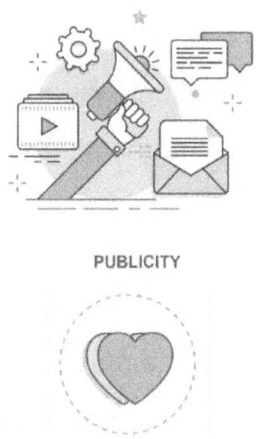

PUBLICITY

 Staff

I.   Personnel requirements for advertising

Check whether more personnel is required for advertising (including graphics) or whether the advertising tasks should or can still be performed by the user.

If there is a need for personnel, the task of assigning employees is created. Job descriptions are an important instrument for this.

Target group

I. Does the advertising reach the target group?

Check whether the advertisement actually reaches the target group or whether the advertisement should be changed.

Examples:

- Market Research
- Surveys at the end of the purchase
- Derivation of data of a buyer which come about with the purchase
- Evaluation of the buyer's origin pages (with several channels such as affiliate marketing)

6.8 Objectives for advertising and communication

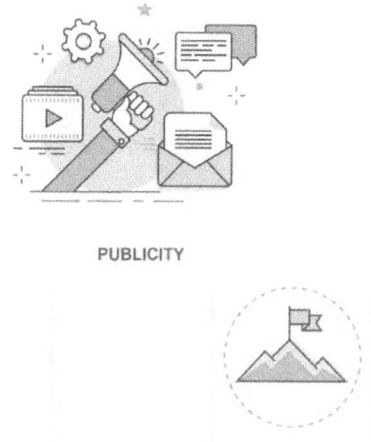

PUBLICITY

I. Objectives for advertising and communication

An important goal of advertising is effectiveness and efficiency.

Effectiveness means getting the desired benefit through the applied method. Efficiency means to be as successful as possible with the effort given.

In order to redefine and check effectiveness and efficiency again and again, one should use important key figures.

Examples:

- Click rates
- Opening rate/feedback rate after advertising campaigns etc.

Basically, the aim of advertising is to make a product/service known or to remind people of the product, to build up an image and or to trigger an action (e.g. The purchase of goods). This is intended to increase turnover and market share.

The point of advertising is a point in the 4P of marketing (advertising policy or communication policy). This means that advertising is, among other things, an important point of contact between the company and the customer. As mentioned above, it is essential for the success of a company that the target group sees the advertising.

II. Objective according to the SMART formula (see 2.8.I.)

Each planned advertising campaign should have its Personal objective. The objective, according to SMART helps to formulate these correctly, to check them again and to pay attention to the scheduling.

Examples of advertising campaigns:

- AdWords campaign
- influencer campaign
- Amazon marketing service campaign
- Etc.

For repetition:

Time and time planning play an important role here, as they form the basis for measuring advertising success alongside the type and scope of the campaign. By measuring the advertising success (or failure), possible improvements should be included in the future planning.

III. Goal of communication

The definition of successful communication is to be understood. Successful communication is so important because misunderstood or insufficiently communicated orders can cost a lot of time and money. An example are gig-workers or other freelancers, who do work of short duration and are often only needed for a few or even individual projects. As these are not part of the company, important information about the company that is decisive for the order cannot be assumed and must be communicated in a special way.

If all relevant content is provided, the goal of successful communication can be achieved sooner. Images, graphics, patterns, examples and objects of comparison (bench partners) can also help to better convey one's Personal thoughts/intentions, as people usually associate different images with different words.

a) Checklists

Checklists can be helpful to communicate all relevant data. These can be adapted to the respective situation if necessary. Below are two examples of checklists:

(a) Example of coffee beans for relevant logo design content

Checklist items	Description
Brand	A piece of heaven
Articles/services	Coffee beans
Material	Arabica Beans
Quality	High quality
Function/Benefit (product-related)	Whole beans to grind yourself
Additional benefits (customer-related)	Particularly digestible; suitable for people with sensitive stomachs (see manufacturing)
Design	The special packaging design is intended to convey the high quality of the product and is also available as a gift.
USP (competitive advantage)	Fair Trade; from the Himalayas; easily digestible
Parties	Coffee farmers; employees who order picking

Fabrication	Fair cultivation, gentle roasting
Location	The beans come from the mountain slopes of the Himalaya Mountains
Slogan	Comes almost from heaven, for heavenly pleasure
Other	Fair trade
Colors & design elements	Green, Gold
Website	Specify if available. Keyword: Corporate Design - otherwise adapt the website later to the elements of the logo. The creation of the entire corporate design could make sense here.
Contents of the order	Logo, if necessary Corporate Design
Comparative objects	Pictures, website, etc.
Please note	Elements of description. Output format: vector graphics and PNG

Etc.	...

(b) Example of the creation of an advertising campaign for a café

Checklist items	Description
Brand/Company name	Dana's Cafe
Articles/services	Café with bakery
Material	Ingredients from regional suppliers
Quality	High quality
Function/Benefit (product-related)	Café as gastronomy and high-quality bakery products to take away
Additional benefits (customer-related)	A "cozy" place to spend time
Design	The baked goods are beautifully decorated.
USP (competitive advantage)	The café design offers a cozy atmosphere and quiet seating niches.
Parties	High quality in a cozy atmosphere and best location (combination of benefits, additional benefits and location)

Fabrication	Family-owned company
Location	Own, fresh production (no frozen bakery products)
Logo	Centrally located in YYY
Slogan	The logo will be sent with the order description.
Target	Still no slogan - is component of this order
Contents of the order	Regional awareness
comparative objects	Banner, flyer, further material, strategy to become known regionally, all data printable in CMYK
Please note	Pictures, website, etc.
Etc.	

A description as accurate as possible should be documented. Many gig platforms offer a satisfaction guarantee. In order to invoke the guarantee, you should document the communication with the service provider (e.g. Save e-mail traffic; screenshots). In addition, one should always ask whether the order has been understood. Especially for foreign gig-workers, it should be clarified that the rights for the work to be created (copyrights) are also required.

 **For service providers**

If the company is to lead to success, it is indispensable for service providers to understand their customers precisely. If a customer does not communicate clearly, it is important to ask questions. Your Personal checklists can help you not to forget anything and always keep an overview of the order.

6.9 Improvement in advertising

PUBLICITY

I. Improvement possibilities for Personal advertising

It can be helpful to keep looking for new ways to advertise that you haven't had in mind before.

Examples:

- Market research - analyzing the market to minimize wastage
- Guerilla marketing
- Sponsoring

- Sales promotion - additional and/or exceptional measures to influence customers
- PR - Press releases
- Improvement of conversation techniques
- Benchmarking

a) Market research

Simply described, the methods of market research consisted of observation and survey. Market research is about better understanding potential customers. If the customer is better understood, wastage can be minimized.

Surveys can be carried out online, in writing, as an interview, etc. Market research can be carried out by internal company personnel or can be outsourced (usually to market research agencies).

Market research, which is aimed directly at customers and actively observes, surveys or even conducts market tests "outside", is called primary research or "field research". Market research that is conducted from a desk and uses existing data is called secondary research or "desk research".

Surveys can simply be carried out freely, e.g. at the information stand using the feedback forms.

Observations can be collected and analyzed, e.g. through behavior in test markets or also in the laboratory - a room in which test persons, for example, perform a product test and are observed.

Improving market research

Market research can be improved by external consultants. For founders, it can make sense to concentrate on the actual core competencies. Market research agencies that deal with the topic of market research on a full-time basis can save the company nerves and time.

For founders who would like to expand their Personal know-how in the field of market research, further training could be helpful. For example, the Udemy platform offers high-quality courses. Under the keyword "market research", courses for start-up market research are available (currently only in English - as of the beginning of 2019), which can be used to improve one's Personal skills. Udemy also offers good courses for various other areas, which can help founders to improve or deepen individual areas (e.g. Online marketing, accounting, etc.).

b) The interview

The interview is a very frequently used tool in surveys.

An interview must be carefully planned in the VorField in order to get the answer to the question asked (in order to deepen the subject of the interview even more, one can further educate oneself with the help of various books, YouTube videos and training courses). External service providers can make interviews completely.

Three example forms of interviews

- The personal interview
- The online interview
- The telephone interview [35]

---

[35] Cf. Altobelli (2017): 56.

c) Press releases (PR, Public Relation)

Public relations, also PR, can be a decisive aid for the success of a company. The aim of PR is to draw the attention of the target group to the company or the product/service. In cooperation with the media, PR can fall back on a multitude of possibilities. [36]Press releases can easily be distributed as press releases. As a rule, however, over 95% of press releases are ignored, so it is important to consider good ideas for the information to be published. Another possibility for PR can be interviews. [37]Interviews can also be bought. A large number of radio or podcast shows can already be reached via influencer platforms.

d) Improving your Personal processes through benchmarking

Benchmarking is an effective instrument of competitive analysis and stands for learning by example - learning by looking.

---

[36] Cf. Ali (2001): 6+7.

[37] Cf. Ali (2001): 42.

The Personal enterprise is compared with a Best Practice enterprise in order to recognize the weak points of the Personal enterprise. The aim is to learn from the "benchmark partner" and thus derive improvement measures.

Benchmarking means the (cross-industry) search for role models in order to compare their strategies, processes, methods but also services/products with one's own.

Steps:

1. Selection of the object - an object can be in this case: product, service, website, process, etc.

2. Selection of the benchmark partner - the comparison company. The prerequisite is that the selected company is better/more exemplary in relation to the selected object.

3. Data collection - data published by companies, newspaper reports, advertisements, activities on the web and in social networks, etc.

4. Identify their Personal weaknesses (found by the comparison) and possible causes.

5. To define and carry out the improvement steps for their Personal products/services.

Types of benchmarking are, among others:

1. Internal benchmarking - comparisons within the company.

2. Competitive benchmarking - comparing "benchmark partners" in the same industry, regardless of whether the same market is served or not.

3. Cross-market benchmarking - comparison of organizational areas or functions/processes, for example. [38]

4. Best practice benchmarking - there are no restrictions in the choice of the "benchmark partner". Exemplary processes, etc. can also be copied in other areas and integrated into your Personal company.

---

[38] Cf. Gerster / Reuter (2013): 48.

3.8 Field 7 - Human

HUMAN

7.4 The legal framework for staff and target group

HUMAN

 **Staff**

I. Legal framework for staff

The law in many respects regulates dealing with personnel.

Examples:

- Employment contracts: What duties/rights arise?
- What is the legal framework for the employment of free-lancers?

- Which laws must be observed (e.g. Maternity Protection Act in Germany)?
- Remuneration regulations
- Pay attention to bogus self-employment of potential free-lancers

a) Rights and obligations under the employment contract

An employment contract is concluded between two parties, the employer and the employee. A contract regulates the relationship between the parties. An employment contract usually contains rights and obligations for both the employee and the employer.

For example, the employer is obliged to pay wages or salaries and, if necessary, to provide materials needed to perform the work. In return for the remuneration, the employer has the right to demand work for the agreed periods. As secondary obligations under the employment contract, there are, for example, the employee's duty of care, the duty of general treatment and also the duty to protect the employee in the best possible way.

The employee has the duty to perform his service at the agreed times. He has the right to receive his remuneration and the right to vacation or breaks. In addition, the employee also has secondary obligations under the employment contract, e.g. fiduciary duty towards the employer.

b) Termination, protection against dismissal and warning

In some countries, there are periods of notice for dismissals, for which possible protection against dismissal laws must be observed. Periods of notice must be observed in all cases.

c) Warnings

A warning is a written disapproval of an employee's conduct. Depending on the severity of the offense, a dismissal in the VorField requires one or more warnings. Warnings are also recorded in the personnel file. In the case of serious breaches of duty, a notice of termination can also become effective without a warning.

d) Termination of the employment relationship

An employment relationship can end in different ways.

Examples:

A fixed-term employment contract: If a fixed-term employment contract is not extended, it is terminated at the end of the employment relationship.

The resignation. If a dismissal is lawful, it also terminates an employment relationship.

A termination agreement usually governs the termination of an employment contract with the consent and agreement of both parties. [39]

 Target audience

II. Legal aspects of dealing with/contacting the target group

---

[39] Cf. Collier (2016): 255.

Dealing with the target group also has various legal regulations.

Examples:

- Consent for e-mail campaigns (country-specific required)
- Is telephone advertising allowed?
- How can the target group be approached in principle?

7.5 Platforms for personnel and target group

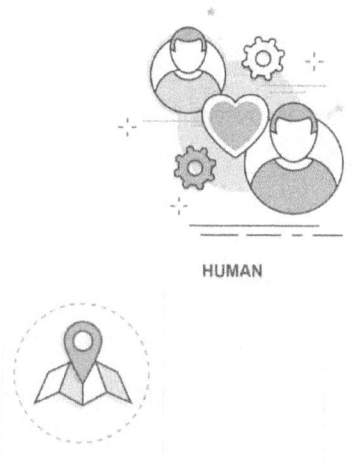

HUMAN

 Staff

I.   Platforms/locations to meet staffing needs

According to the definition in this book, job exchanges form platforms to meet staffing needs.

Example:

- Indeed
- Monsters

- Regional newspapers

 Target audience

II. Further places where the target group can be found

The aim here is to find platforms on which the target group is on the move, which at first glance do not offer any sales or advertising. Facebook does not offer a sales opportunity, but it does offer advertising. The platforms found can offer advantages, e.g. that through sponsoring, indirect advertising can be done quickly and inexpensively.

Example:

- Blogs/Communities
- Meeting of "communities" e.g. Congress of Forest kindergartens, Meeting of alternative thinking families, Whisky tasting, ..

7.6 Recruiting employees and the advertising message

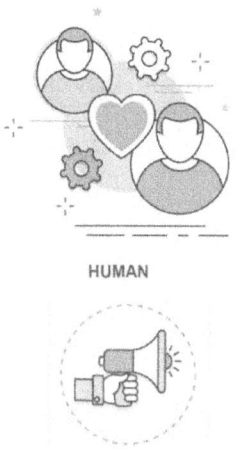

HUMAN

 Staff

I. Recruiting employees

In times of boom and boom it can be difficult to get suitable employees. It is therefore important to offer an advantage to other employers and to communicate this to them.

Example:

Employer branding

Employer branding is an employer brand. An employer brand conveys a positive image of the company to the applicant. The employer brand offers many advantages: Applicants like to come and can be selected from a large number. However, an employer brand is difficult for small companies to implement. However, a fair, positive overall picture of the company can create a similar smaller form of employer brand, especially regionally.

 Target group

I. Advertising messages for the target group

A quote by Martin Walser underlines the relevance of the fact that advertising statements have to be checked for the target group's understanding: "Man is not who he is, but who he wants to be. Whoever grabs him by his wishes, has him".

Do the advertising messages really meet the target group's wishes?

Examples of the test:

- Which feelings are addressed by the advertising statements 1.6?
- Which terms are used?
- What does the target group associate with the terms?
- What is the general definition of the terms? - This can be found out through market research (e.g. Surveys).

It is important to check the advertising messages in relation to the target group. Words, symbols and terms are perceived differently by different customer segments (e.g. The colloquial language of customers under 30 and customers over 60).

Advertising messages are often the first encounter between customer and product/service, and thus contribute significantly to the decision whether the customer is thinking in the direction of a decision to purchase or use the service.

The feelings that the customer associates with the advertising message are replaced by the experience with the product/service after the purchase of the product/service.

An important feeling, which should appear at least briefly with the customer, is luck. For example, if the customer eats his burger, he should feel pleasure and happiness. Through this experience the customer probably comes back and can become a part of the customer base.

An example from the service/garden care: If a customer sees his freshly cut hedge, he should feel lucky. The same applies here: This experience can cause the customer to commission further services.

A product/service should therefore always convince through quality and clean work.

7.8 Objectives for staff and target group

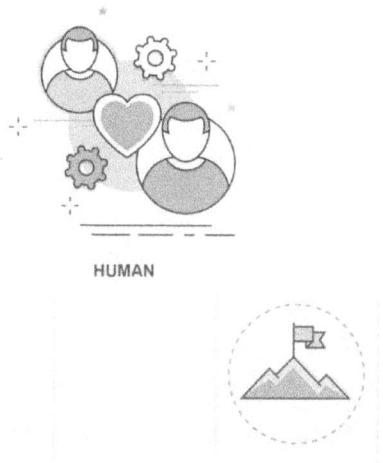

HUMAN

 Staff

I.   Goals with employees

As a rule, companies pursue the goal of countering growth with their employees. Further goals have to be defined and adjusted if necessary.

Examples:

- Divide work, e.g. for your Personal relief.

- Employees who understand the goals of the company and develop them independently.
- Gaining know-how/competencies for the company
- Bring "new wind" into the company

a) Analysis of application documents

The analysis of application documents is not only about whether the applicant is technically suitable, but also about the fact that several conclusions can be drawn from one application.

The evaluation of the application documents can, for example, be carried out on the basis of three scales. Depending on the requirements, a certain number of minus points can lead to a rejection, a certain number of plus points to an invitation to an interview.

	+	+/-	-
Complete documents			
....			

Examples of criteria for the application documents:

o Completeness of the documents

o Scope of documents

o Design of the documents

Examples of curriculum vitae criteria:

o Completeness

o Current professional activity

o school background

o Career history

o Professional experience

o Reason for application (if recognizable)

o Time gaps in the curriculum vitae

o Development of the applicant

o Voluntary work

Examples of criteria in the cover letter:

o Is there a reference to the job description?

o Is the reason for the application recognizable?

o What is the linguistic structure?

o What is the structure?

o Is the applicant convincing?

Examples of criteria in the certificates:

o Is there a red thread?

o Is specialist knowledge available?

o Course of school education

o Course of vocational training

o Work performance (from job references) [40]

Criteria can also be weighted individually.

----

[40] Cf. Tietze (2002): 134 ff.

b) Controlling the cost-benefit of personnel development

As stated in the Introduction to Personnel Development, personnel development is about ensuring that current and future tasks/work can be done as effectively as possible.

A cost-benefit analysis deals with how high the benefits and the costs are for a possible development/expansion of the personnel.

A rough key figure can provide the calculation of profitability. In the same way, calculation methods that appear to be suitable can be independently deepened here. The economic efficiency of personnel development can be roughly calculated using the formula:

Yield: Expenses

This involves planned income and the planned total expenditure. Not only gross wages, but also ancillary wage costs must be taken into account in personnel development. Possible placement fees for skilled workers can also be added.

If the result is less than 1, this is a negative indication for the planned development.

If the result is multiplied by 100, the result is the percentage of profitability.

Example:

Yield = 30,000

Expense = 20,000

The result is 1.5 and therefore positive. Expressed as a percentage, this is 150%. In this rough example, the personnel development and the orders accepted as a result pay off. Of course, decisions cannot only be based on this formula. There are equally important jobs in companies that do not pay for themselves immediately and that improve the image. Thus a countervalue is possibly not immediately visible.

 Target audience

II. Objectives for the target group

For the target group an objective is very meaningful. By defining the objective, partial objectives can be created and controlled and, if necessary, adapted.

Example:

Define what percentage of the target group is to be reached (this percentage, thus becomes a key figure). Here, too, a percentage that is as accurate as possible and a timely milestone is important in order to steer or control goals.

7.9 Improvement for staff and target group

HUMAN

 Target audience

I. Improvement in dealing with the target audience

Since the customer is at the center of the company, it is always important to look for ways to improve communication.

Example:

Integrate a CRM system. CRM stands for Customer Relationship Management. The CRM system is a very good way to improve the handling of the target audience. In itself, CRM can also be seen as part of advertising, as it influences the customer's opinion.

A CRM system is equally suitable for a manufacturing and a service industry.

 Employees

I. Improving communication with employees

The 4-eared model according to Schulz von Thun (Book tip: Talking together: 1; von Schulz von Thun) can improve communication with employees.

a) The communication model

The communication model / communication square or also the 4-ear model after the psychologist Friedemann Schulz von Thun says that a message has 4 sides. The 4 pages indicate 4 possibilities how a message can be expressed and recorded.

The 4 pages are:

- The subject level
- The Spell
- The relationship level
- The self-denunciation

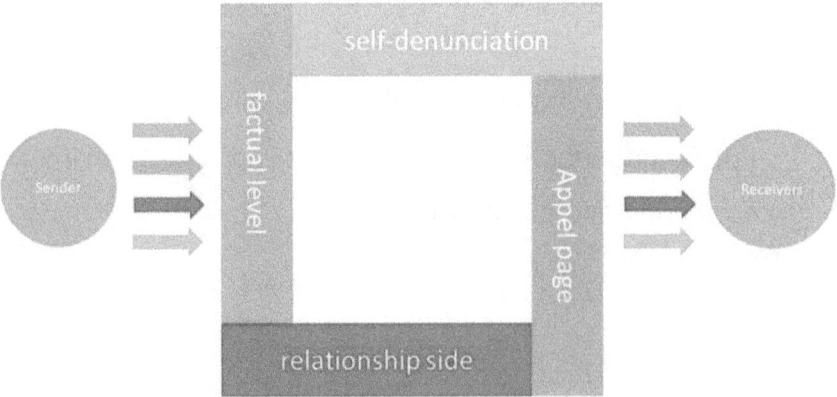

Figure 44 – 4- Ear model after Schulz von Thun

This results in various possibilities how a message can be recorded. For example, a subject message is not automatically recorded at the subject level.

The aim of the communication square is to show that communication can also be misunderstood. Misunderstandings can originate from the sender as well as from the receiver.

If the sender of a message is aware of this, communication can take place in a more targeted manner. When listening to (negative) aspects in a message, the recipient of a message should also ask himself whether the message is really meant as (negative) as he heard it.

Communication helps to eliminate communication problems. Thus, purposeful asking can create clarity.[41]

---

[41] Cf. Schulz von Thun (2013):16 ff.

3.9 Field 8 – Goal

GOAL

GOAL

I. Legal framework for objectives/control/controlling including accounting

The entire accounting system, which is a component of controlling, is strictly regulated in many countries, since taxes and other levies must be paid to the state and the state can check the taxes to be paid more uniformly through a strictly regulated accounting system.

Examples of legal regulations in accounting:

- Annual financial statements
- Profit and loss account
- Proper bookkeeping
- Legal framework for accounting - general
- Legal framework for insolvencies
- Legal framework for REWE - Taxes
- Revenue surplus accounts

II.   Examples of generally important principles

These "principles" are usually important for every company. Irrespective of the country in which the business is carried out. It is indispensable for every company to observe country-specific rights, as non-observance leads to major problems.

1. Correctness and arbitrariness

- Postings must be traceable
- Postings must actually have taken place.

2. Clarity and rationality

The structure of the accounts must be clear, concise and orderly so that the accounts are easily readable by an expert third party.

3. Completeness

The accounts must be complete and complete.

4. Document principle

Transactions must be supported by supporting documents

III.   Annual accounts

In the case of small entrepreneurs, in some countries it is sufficient to submit a surplus income statement for the annual accounts.

A profit and loss account is the simplest basis for carefully preparing the annual accounts. Careful execution is important not only for the state in question, but also for the company itself. E.g. through an EÜR expense and income become visible, from this conclusion can be derived which are important components for the controlling.

Below is a simplified presentation of the EÜR without taking VAT into account.

Operating revenues	Total
	...
Sum	100.000
Operating expenses	
	...
Sum	-10.000
Annual surplus	
Operating revenues	100.000
Operating expenses	-10.000
Gain	90.000

In many countries, larger companies need a balance sheet and a profit and loss account for their annual financial statements. These and other legal regulations must be observed and planned. In case of doubt, professional help is required.

8.5 Platforms for controllers and key areas

GOAL

I.   Platforms for controllers

Which platforms are relevant for controllers? This point gains importance when controlling is performed internally. If the entire accounting department is outsourced, the tax consultant usually takes over this point.

Examples:

- Communities for controllers

In this course, platforms are also understood to mean software programs that simplify controlling throughout the entire company:

- Software for accounting
- Software for invoices
- Software for merchandise management (merchandise management systems, e.g. SAP)

The great advantage of software programs is that key figures can be read out quickly.

8.6 Communication strategy for controlling

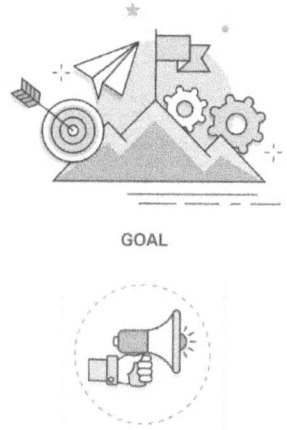

GOAL

I. Communication strategy for goals, control and controlling

If objectives are monitored, they must be communicated to the project participants. A hidden check can make a negative impression on employees (permanent employees or freelancers) and create a picture of non-confidence. With the right communication, controlling becomes easier.

Even too much control can demotivate employees and inhibit a relationship of trust.

Regular communication of the goals themselves is just as important. Only those who know the goals can help to implement them.

8.7 Target audience and personnel for controlling

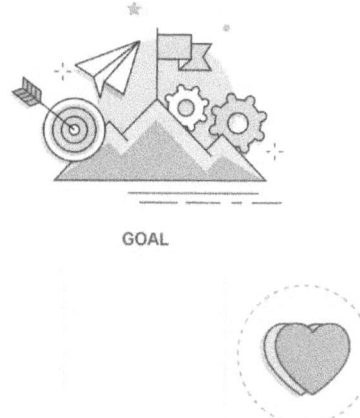

GOAL

 Target audience

I. Persons for whom Controlling data is relevant

Depending on who is the target audience for controlling, the data must be worked out accordingly. Banks and investors can probably do more with appealing explanatory graphics; tax offices need corresponding information according to strict guidelines.

Examples:

- Investors
- Banks
- Tax offices
- In the case of project management, the managing director/supervisor
- Clients
- Executive boards

 Staff

II. Personnel requirements with controlling

Define and plan the personnel requirements/expenses associated with objectives, accounting and controlling.

If necessary, assign employees or check whether the tasks can be done by yourself (depending on time, knowledge and ability).

8.9 Improvement for the controlling/accounting system

GOAL

I. Improvement of controlling / target setting

Define how the controlling/objective can be improved. Innovations, whether through models or IT solutions, can potentially facilitate work and save money.

Example:

- Setting milestones to subdivide the objective more concretely

- Clarify target definitions. Market research (better knowledge of the target audience based on concrete figures), for example, can contribute to this. If experiences arise, target definitions should be adapted (for the next time window).

- Expansion of the key performance indicator system

- Attend controller training courses/enable employees to participate

- Keep an eye out for new IT solutions for this sector

- Use of existing models to better measure facts. Some models have already been mentioned in this book. There are countless instruments, models, etc. for strategic and operational needs. These can be searched e.g. by Google searches or also management books for the respective enterprise suitably.

3.10 Field 9 - Improvement

IMPROVEMENT

9.4 The legal framework for improvements and innovation

IMPROVEMENT

I. Defining the legal side effects of possible improvements and innovations

Especially when a company is already running, there is often the risk that changes or new products "simply" flow into it. The necessity of a review, especially with regard to the legal framework, is no longer present at this point.

Therefore, the advice is never to lose sight of the legal framework in order not to offer an additional target.

Examples and countermeasures:

- Unconscious infringement of third-party rights such as patents, brand names, domains or even advertising slogans.
- This can be counteracted by carrying out comprehensive research or commissioning a search for improvements and innovations.
- Change in the basis of product liability
- Here it must be examined whether improvements or innovation also changes changes with regard to product liability.
- Particularly in the case of innovations or fundamental improvements, the following should be examined:

Are there any possibilities of applying for new, further Personal rights, e.g. in the form of patents, utility models, rights for domains or design protection?

9.5 Platforms to improve or innovate

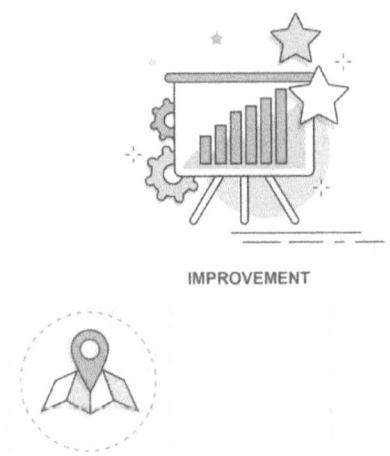

IMPROVEMENT

I.　Platforms to improve or innovate

Depending on the industry, there are various platforms that can help to improve products or services. These platforms can be used for new products, but also for optimizations. By nature, the external search for improvements would be seen as consulting. This results in the keyword "consulting". Freelance consultants can also contribute to innovation. Improvements and innovations may create great chances of profit and should therefore not be ignored. In times of growing Gig-Econmomy (freelance workers hired for "Gigs"), the potential of freelance employees to get support in innovation search is growing.

Examples of platforms:

- Websites for contests/competitions/tenders/innovation search (e.g.:https://www.baunetz.de/wettbewerbe/wettbewerb_index_auslobungen_94091.html)
- Website for Gig Workers

(E.g.: https://www.dnxjobs.de/ and as mentioned in Field 6: fiverr.com, designenlassen.de, etc.)

II. Platforms for improving (general) entrepreneurial activity

Internal and external platforms can use data to help enable comprehensive analysis and identify clues for improvement.

Examples of internal platforms (sources):

- The company's Personal merchandise management system

- The company's Personal production data acquisition system

- IT systems (information technology)

IT systems / databases specially designed for the company or "simply" self-created Excel directories: The aim is to capture, store and make accessible knowledge with the aim of laying the foundation for improvements and optimizations through documentation and the creation of links.

Examples of external platforms (sources):

- Research Institutes
- Libraries (BS)

9.6 Advertising with innovations

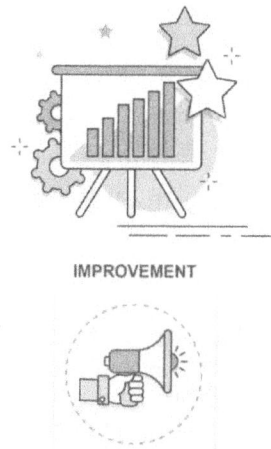

IMPROVEMENT

I.   Finding out advertising possibilities with innovations & Co.

Innovations, improvements or optimizations can, if they bring real benefits, bring advertising potential with them. This benefit must also be communicated (as described in Field 1.6). Design awards can underline the "new" quality, and greatly enhance a product.

Examples:

- Special advertising campaigns relating to innovation or improvement
- Design awards, creative industry awards for innovations, for example:

  o Red Dot Design Award https://www.red-dot.org/de

  o German Design Award https://www.german-design-award.com/

9.7 Improvement through Target audience and employees

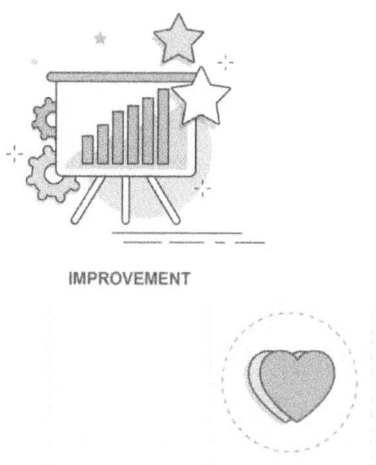

IMPROVEMENT

 Target audience

I. Persons contributing to improvement and innovation identification

Various people can contribute to the improvement in the company. Once the groups have been identified, measures can be planned and implemented for them.

Examples:

- Clients
- Staff
- Partner companies
- Counselor
- Freelancers

 Staff

I. Methods how employees can contribute ideas to improve

There are, among other things, the following options for integrating employees when finding ideas for improving the product/service.

The "customer" is in a special position here. For him, methods such as questioning and observation are more suitable in order to integrate his opinion into products if necessary.

Examples of creativity techniques:

a) Brainstorming

Brainstorming collects ideas on a given topic and divides them into categories.

The basic recommendation for the group size is 5 - 8 persons.

Suggestions/ideas are written on index cards - one card per idea. The cards have the advantage that they can be easily sorted on a pinboard/magnetic board, for example. All ideas are allowed. When brainstorming, care should be taken not to criticize participants for their ideas.

b) Brainwriting / 6-3-5 method

This method is similar to brainstorming. However, the ideas/suggestions are recorded in written form. The method is, therefore "silent" and does not require any great moderation. Also, here, negative comments are not allowed.

In the 6-3-5 method, 6 participants write down 3 ideas and pass them on 5 times. The successor expands the ideas of the predecessors in the 2nd - 6th step.[42]

1st idea TN 1	Further develop-ment of the succes-sor of the idea de-scribed by TN 1	...	...	...	...
2nd idea TN 1	...	...	...	...	...
3rd idea TN 3	...	...	...	...	...

c) Mind-Mapping

In mind mapping, a construct is formed from connections around a main theme. As a rule, mind mappings are designed on a whiteboard or similar.

The mind mapping method offers the great advantage that connections and resulting subtopics are clearly visible. From this a kind of dynamic is mapped. Of course, a mind map can also be displayed graphically on the PC.

---

[42] . Backerra, Malorny, Schwarz 2007: 79 f.

9.8 Goals for improvement and innovation

IMPROVEMENT

I. Defining the goals for improvement and innovation

Improvement and innovation can bring many advantages if all factors are taken into account and the calculation is correct. It is also important to set goals for improvements and innovations. Those who do not know their goals cannot achieve them. The achievement of goals can be measured by key figures (e.g. Duration of a production/work flow) but also by surveys of the target audience.

Examples why improvement and innovation can be important:

- The target audience can be extended
- The target audience can be further satisfied
- Customers can be better bound to the company
- The company remains current
- Resources can be saved (e.g. Through new machines)
- Company expansion possible
- If necessary, reasons for a subcontractor
- The product life cycle can be extended

4 <u>Further Application of the Matrix</u>

4.1 Subsequent Changes

An example of how to deal with subsequent changes (here introduction of a CRM system) on the basis of the matrix in the area of improvement in the handling of the target audience:

CRM stands for Customer Relationship Management. A CRM system is (usually) equally important for a manufacturing and a service industry.

Before CRM is introduced into the company, it is checked by the six practical fields.

§	What legal aspects need to be considered when introducing CRM? Example: • - Data Protection Act
	Are there already ready-made platforms that help to easily integrate CRM into the company? Internet research shows that there are already many providers who offer ready-made software for customer care or CRM. The wheel does not have to be reinvented here and the use of the existing

	know-how can save a lot of time and money at this point.
	1 The CRM offers advertising possibilities, because customers can be sent an email on birthdays, for example, and the company can thus be positively brought into awareness. 2. How is the CRM to communicate to the employees of the company? With a CRM it is important that the employees implement it. If they do not use it or only hardly use it, it is practically non-existent. Communication and the communication of goals are very important for this.
	Which goals are pursued with CRM? Example: - 10% increase in sales in the next quarter by existing customers • - 30 % less migration of customers to the competition in the next 12 months

	What opportunities for improvement are there with CRM? Example: - Inclusion of suppliers in the CRM system • - 100 % compliance with the internally planned handling of CRM

Of course, the practical part of checking the introduction of the CRM system can be further refined. This procedure only serves as a basic explanation.

4.2 Further example of a sub-matrix - competition analysis

A sub-matrix can refine the regular analysis, but can also bring repetition.

The competitive analysis as a sub-matrix with one example:

	To what extent does the Personal service differ from the services of the three largest competitors? (In order to know who the company's competitors are, it is necessary to search for similar products/services and thus find the respective manufacturers/providers. The competition from service providers tends to be regional, that of products mostly supra-regional. (Similar products/services can be searched for on the platforms on which services or products are sold, but also by visiting (specialist) shops or, in the case of regional recognition, by inspecting signs, advertising on vehicles, etc.)

	What strategy is the competition pursuing?
	What is the estimated turnover of the competition?
	Does the competition have patents, trademark applications, etc.?
	Where does the competition offer its product/service?
	What does the competition advertise with?
	How many employees does the competition employ? Who is the target audience of the competition?

GOAL	What are the main goals of the competition?
IMPROVEMENT	Does the competition have products/services that are particularly innovative?

4.3 What remains at the end of the Entrepreneur Matrix?

At the end, i.e. after the company has completely worked through the matrix, the basic thinking module of the matrix should have found its way into the user's system.

With the 9 symbols and the practical experience that each field explains itself by the other fields, the user can create his Personal matrices for each problem of the company and thus gain an overview. A matrix is also very well suited for brainstorming before the company is founded.

A suggestion for the personal documentation of a company would be to divide the Entrepreneur Matrix folder into the following parts:

1) The planning phase: A folder with three files. The 3 files consist of FIELD 1-3 and form the foundation, the theory.

2. The implementation phase: a folder with six files. The files consist of FIELD 4-9.

3. The improvements: Any number of matrices. New entries are checked/implemented on the basis of the five steps.

4. All submatrices

5. Empty templates: This folder should contain empty templates for improvements, submatrices and the general matrix (three elements). New questions, theories and models should always be entered to be up to date with all improvements.

5 The matrix as a business plan

A document that no entrepreneur can avoid is a business plan.

The business plan is the plan that represents the company's future actions.

A business plan is a classic document for submission to banks, investors or crowdfunding.

After working through the contents, the matrix is so profound that it can provide all the information required for a business plan. The business plan described below makes use of the information already developed from the matrix. The information listed below can be expanded and completed according to bank requirements. The matrix business plan is much more comprehensive than the typical bank document.

The business plan can and should be an accompanying, documenting and thus stable foundation for the company through updating and adaptation.

I. External form

Before drawing up the business plan, it should be clarified which external form one chooses. There is no uniform form. Depending on the donor, other styles may be preferred.

Examples:

- How should the business plan be drawn up? Keyword or formulated?
- In what time (present or future) should the business plan be drawn up?
- Should the business plan be written in a personal (I) or general (man) form?
- Should there be a cover page with the bank's title as with an application?
- Is a new page chosen for each heading?
- Which headings and structure points, in which order, should there be in the business plan?

II.   The summary idea

(In business administration also called Executive-Summary)

The summary should be about one to two A4 pages long. Although it appears at the beginning of the business plan, it is only written at the end of the business plan, as it is a summary.

It can be useful to have an expert look at the finished business plan before submitting it to investors and banks.

On the Internet you will find many different templates (good and not so good, evaluations can help to make a suitable selection) for executive summaries.

III.   The product / service description

Information explaining the product/service must be provided. In addition to texts, pictures, graphics or objects of comparison may also be useful.

To be found in matrix field: 1.2

IV. Strategy

Describe the selected strategies for production/production.

Example

- Make or buy
- Personal or third-party bearings

To be found in matrix field: 2.1

V. Finances

Depending on the chosen strategy, the financing require-ments, sales, profits, contribution margin, etc. are to be de-scribed here. On the Internet there are various repayment cal-culators (in order to find a calculator that is as faithful as pos-sible, you should also pay attention to valuations here) with which installments can be calculated. For banks, the consid-eration of these factors usually makes a positive impression.

A planned P&L/EUR can also be submitted. Here, future ex-penses and income are professionally compared.

For banks and investors, the Personal contribution in this field must also be described.

To be found in matrix field: Field 3; 2.3; 1.3

VI.   Description of the company

The chosen type of company (with justification) should be mentioned here.

The thoroughly analyzed competition should also be included in the business plan. It can be transferred from the information developed in Matrix Field 2.4. A SWOT analysis has a professional effect and helps to show the potential lender that opportunities and risks are taken into account.

To be found in matrix field: 2.4

VII.   Positioning and sales platforms

The positioning should be justified in this field. The market participants (other providers and target audiences) should be considered for the justification. Accordingly, sales platforms (online and offline) should be named and access possibilities to them described (usually through contracts). If there are barriers, consideration should be given to ways in which the product/service can still be offered.

Example: Many sales platforms want to advertise with the product. Not all products are accepted on all sales platforms or retail shops. The consideration of the possibility to take this hurdle would be to contact the respective platforms in advance and get a temporary okay.

To be found in matrix field: 2.5

VIII.   Advertising strategy

Defining and describing the advertising strategy and the associated media and carriers.

To be found in matrix field: 2.6

IX.   Human Structure

A detailed profile of the founder should be created here. Possible employees should also be described. If there are employees, the organization of these should be determined, e.g. by an organization chart.

To be found in matrix field: 2.7 for startup

X.   Objective

The objectives should define operational and strategic goals. Milestones can show the potential lender that the project has been dealt with in detail. It is important to have a well planned target description, e.g. according to the SMART criteria.

To be found in matrix field: 2.8

XI.   Risk catalogue

A risk catalogue, e.g. based on the matrix structure, helps to show that one has dealt extensively with risks. As a (new) entrepreneur, it is very important for lenders to deal with risks, since risks for a company could mean a possible default.

To be found in matrix field: Risk Matrix

6 <u>Bibliography</u>

Ali, M. (2001): Public Relations, Munich.

Altobelli, C. F. (2017): Market Research: Methods - Applications - Practical Examples, Stuttgart.

Backerra, H. / Malorny, C. / Schwarz, W. (2007): Creativity techniques: initiating creative processes, promoting innovation, 3rd, completely revised edition, Munich.

Bleiber, R. (2011): Successful start-up, Freiburg

Fleing, E. / Evers, M. (2008): Excellently positioned: how to get customers to find you ; effective self-marketing instead of expensive acquisition ; with the 20 best marketing instruments ; [for start-ups, self-employed and small entrepreneurs], Munich

Finkreißen, A. (1999): Process Value Creation: New Conception of a Model for Benefit-Oriented Analysis and Evaluation, Berlin

Fischer, J. / Unger, W. (2001): Management and Organization, Munich

Gerster, W. / Reuter R. (2013): Logistics controlling with benchmarking: practical examples from industry and trade, Wiesbaden.

Götz, U. (2010): Cost Accounting and Cost Management, Berlin.

Heinen, E. (2013): Industrial Management: Decisions in Industrial Operations, Heidelberg.

Hillmann, M. (2017): The 1x1 of Corporate Communications: A Guide to Practice, Heidelberg

Hingston, P. (2001): Marketing - basic knowledge for the self-employed, Munich

Hofbauer, G. / Sangl, A. (2017): Professional product management: the process-oriented approach, framework conditions and strategies, Weinheim

Intveen, C. (2013): Corporate Strategies of International Automakers: Effects of Transport Policy Commitments on the Corporate Level, Heidelberg

Kiessling, W. / Babel, F. (2016): Corporate Identity: Strategy of sustainable corporate management, Regensburg.

Knop, R. (2009): Success factors of strategic networks of small and medium-sized enterprises: An IT-supported guide to successful cooperation, Heidelberg

Jochem, R. / Giebel, M. (2011): Six Sigma made easy: a text-book with sample project for practical success ; [with 19 method templates to download], Düsseldorf.

Meffert, H. / Burmann, C. / Kirchgeorg, M. (2014): Marketing: Grundlagen marktientierter Unternehmensführung, 12th edition, Wiesbaden.

Niermeyer, R. (2006): Coaching: Developing goals, strengthening self-confidence, monitoring success, Freiburg.

Otto, I. (2008): Container management within the framework of just-in-time concepts, Munich.

Pepels, W. (2013): Practical handbook Relaunch: Making the most of the potential of existing brands, Düsseldorf

Pepels, W. (2017): The 4P in Marketing, Berlin.

Pfläging, N. (1998): Controlling system for strategic and operative planning of international consulting projects: Using the example of energy supply companies with special consideration of the development of an acquisition system, Hamburg.

Plum, B. (1997): Mein Business Plan, Freiburg im Breisgau.

Poth, L. G. / Pradel, M. / Poth, G. S. (2011): Gabler Kompakt-Lexikon Marketing, 3rd edition, Wiesbaden.

Rennhak, C. (2017): Strategic Marketing, Munich.

Rolf, A. (2013): Fundamentals of Organizational and Business Informatics, Heidelberg

Roux, A. (2015): Green Distribution: Evaluation of selected concepts for implementing sustainable distribution, Hamburg.

Schulz von Thun, F. (2013): Talking to each other: 1, Hamburg.

Stamminger, A. (2008): Selected concepts for defining the relevant market and critical assessment, Munich.

Thudium, T. (2015): Technologieorientiertes strategisches Marketing: Die Entwicklung eines neuen Referenzrahmen zur Genierung von Marketingstrategien für technologieorientierte Unternehmen, Heidelberg (Technology-Oriented Strategic Marketing: The Development of a New Reference Framework for the Generation of Marketing Strategies for Technology-Oriented Companies).

Titze, C. (2002): Methods of personality analysis: assessing and selecting people, Tübingen.

Tripp, C. (2019): Distribution and Retail Logistics: Networks and Strategies of Omnichannel Distribution in Retailing, Heidelberg

Von Berkenstein, G. (2011): Economic Handbook of Formulas and Key Figures: Reference book for students and professionals, Berlin

Vry, W. (2017): The examination of marketing specialists, 7th edition, Herne.

Weis, H. C. (2013): Marketing, Herne.

Wolff, C. (2008): Advertising management in young growth companies: An Analysis of the Influence of Advertising Planning and Control on the Success of Young Growth Companies in Consideration of Corporate Development, Heidelberg

Züger, R.-M. (2007): Self-Management - Leadership-Basiskompetenz: theoretical basics and methods with examples, practical tasks, repetition questions and answers, Zurich.

Imprint / Author

Sascha Wlaschek
Alter Hesterkamp 10
32425 Minden
Deutschland
saschawl@yahoo.de

Basement - 1st edition - May 2019

www.basement.rocks

www.ingramcontent.com/pod-product-compliance
Lightning Source LLC
Chambersburg PA
CBHW072130170526
45158CB00004BA/1315